NELSON Language ARTS

AND WHO ARE YOU?

Caren Cameron

Maureen Dockendorf

Betty Eades

Barb Eklund

Christine Finochio

Ruth Hay

Sharon Jeroski

Eugene Mazur

Mary McCarthy

Wayne McNanney

Maureen Skinner

Chris Worsnop

Senior Program Consultant

Jennette MacKenzie

 I(T)P Nelson

an International Thomson Publishing company

Toronto • Albany • Bonn • Boston • Cincinnati • Detroit • London • Madrid • Melbourne
Mexico City • New York • Pacific Grove • Paris • San Francisco • Singapore • Tokyo • Washington

Grade 4 Reviewers:

Lynn Archer
New Westminster, British Columbia

Joyce Billinkoff
Winnipeg, Manitoba

Kerry Black
Calgary, Alberta

Faye Brownbridge
Calgary, Alberta

Mady Davidson
Winnipeg, Manitoba

Maureen Dockendorf
Port Moody, British Columbia

Linda Doody
Clarenville, Newfoundland

Carol Germyn
Calgary, Alberta

Charlotte Henryk
Regina, Saskatchewan

Phyllis Hildebrandt
Ste. Anne, Manitoba

Debra Huitema
Calgary, Alberta

Cheryl Lemire
Calgary, Alberta

Toni Marasco
Calgary, Alberta

Shawn Moynihan
Guelph, Ontario

Linda Nosbush
Prince Albert, Saskatchewan

Marilyn Raman
Winnipeg, Manitoba

Heather Weber
Whitby, Ontario

Shauneen Pete-Willett
Saskatoon, Saskatchewan

Wayne Williams
Clarenville, Newfoundland

Equity Consultant:
Ken Ramphal

I(T)P® International Thomson Publishing
The ITP logo is a trademark under licence
www.thomson.com

Published by
I(T)P® Nelson
A division of Thomson Canada Limited, 1998
1120 Birchmount Road
Scarborough, Ontario M1K 5G4
www.nelson.com

Printed and bound in Canada

4 5 6 7 8 9 0 / ML / 7 6 5 4 3 2 1 0

Canadian Cataloguing in Publication Data

Main entry under title:

Nelson language arts 4

ISBN 0-17-607523-2 (v. 1 : bound)
ISBN 0-17-606606-3 (v. 1 : pbk.)
Contents: [1] And Who Are You?

1. Readers (Elementary). I. Cameron, Caren, 1949–

PE1121.N434 1997   428.6   C97-930958-1

Project Team: Angela Cluer, Mark Cobham, Daryn Dewalt, Kathleen ffolliott, Susan Green, Julie Greener, Liz Harasymczuk, John McInnes, Allan Moon, Ken Phipps, June Reynolds, Elizabeth Salomons, Theresa Thomas, Jill Young

TABLE OF CONTENTS

Unit 3 *Media Close-up* 128

Unit 1: *And Who Are You?*

How would you answer the question, "And Who Are You?"
You could probably come up with all sorts of answers. In this
unit, you'll read about the many ways people and story
characters let you know who *they* are. As you read and talk
about their interests, talents, and ideas, you will think, talk,
and learn more about yourself. You will

- find out about the lives of real people
  and story characters
- think and talk about your own feelings
  and experiences
- tell about yourself and others in pictures,
  letters, stories, and poems
- learn to follow rules for spelling, capitalization,
  punctuation, and sentences
- make a personal collection

I CAN

Written by Mari Evans
Illustrated by Renée Cuthbertson

I can
be anything
I can
do anything
I can
think
anything
big
or tall
OR
high or low
W I D E
or narrow
fast or slow
because I
CAN
and
I
WANT
TO!

9

The Greatest

Written by Michael Rosen
Illustrated by Quentin Blake

I'm the world's greatest at sport
I've won gold medals for
underwater tennis
nose throwing
elbow climbing
potato jumping
snail lifting
and computer wrestling.

I'm the world's greatest inventor
I've invented
a dog scrambler
a sock mixer
a throat cleaner
a mustache toaster
and a custard sprinkler.

I'm the world's greatest.

I WANT TO BE

Written by Thylias Moss
Illustrated by Jerry Pinkney

Today a lady, a man, another lady, another man, and my friend asked me what do I want to be.

I thought and I thought. They were tired of waiting so I said, I'll tell you tomorrow.

I walked home slowly. I kicked up rocks and dirt that filled the air like tiny butterflies. I held a handful of river water. Then I let go of it above my head like rain. I licked a patch of sunlight on my arm. I played hopscotch in footprints after I made them. I made a grass mustache, a dandelion beard, and a bird nest toupee.

LEARNING GOALS

You will

- get to know a girl who imagines what she wants to be

- note how writers use words to create pictures

13

The wind was a magician and it turned me into a dancer. I danced until I was dizzy and the sky turned into a lake so I stood on my head and was a fish swimming in it. I double-dutched with strands of rainbow. Then I fastened the strands to my hair and my toes and became a fiddle that sunbeams played. Then I sang with the oxygen choir.

At sunset I was a firefighter and I squirted water at the sun until it turned into the moon and until it was so dark the stars couldn't play hide-and-seek anymore.

"All home free," I said.

By the time I got home, I knew what I wanted to be.

I want to be big but not so big that a mountain or a mosque or a synagogue seems small. I want to be strong but not so strong that a kite seems weak. I want to be old but not so old that Mars and Jupiter and redwoods seem young. I want to be fast but not so fast that lightning seems slow. I want to be wise but not so wise that I can't learn anything.

I want to be green but not so green that I can't also be purple. I want to be tall but not so tall that nothing is above me. Up must still be somewhere, with clouds and sky.

I want to be quiet but not so quiet that nobody can hear me. I also want to be sound, a whole orchestra with two bassoons and an army of cellos. Sometimes I want to be just the triangle, a tinkle that sounds like an itch.

I want to be still but not so still that I turn into
a mannequin or get mistaken for a tree. I want to be
in motion but I want the ants in my pants to sometimes
take a vacation. Sometimes I want to be slow but not so slow
that everything passes me by.

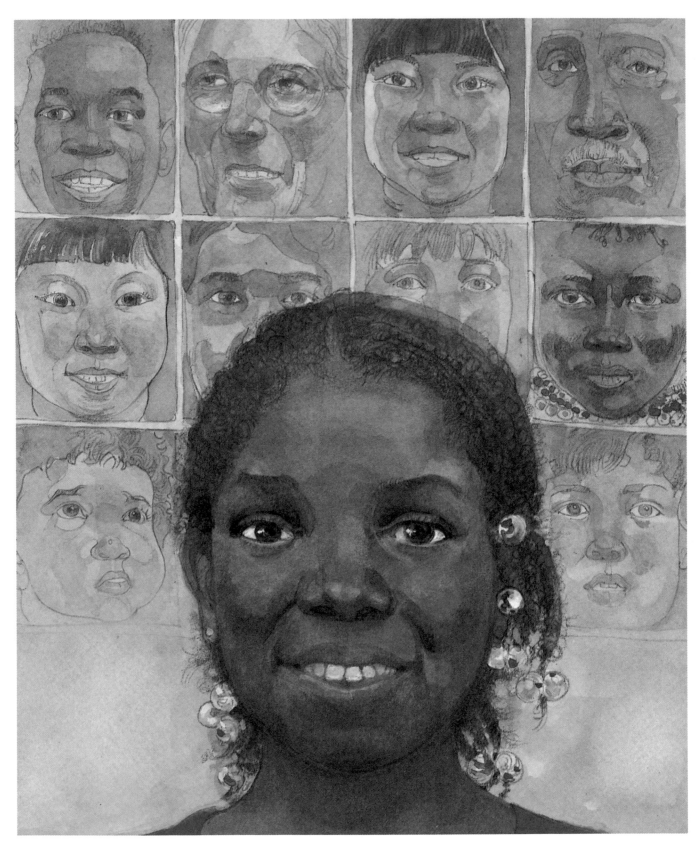

Sometimes I want to be small but not so small that I am easy to miss. About the size of the thought of a bud before it opens and becomes a universe in which bees orbit like planets.

Sometimes I want to be invisible but not gone. Sometimes I want to be weightless and floating on air, able to fly when I want to and able to stay on the ground when I feel like it. I want to be a leaf that is part canoe riding the water as if it's a liquid horse. I want to be comfortable in all the elements.

I want to be all the people I know, then I want to know more people so I can be them too. Then they can all be me.

I want to be a new kind of earthquake, rocking the world as if it's a baby in a cradle.

I want to be eyes looking, looking everywhere. I want to be ears hearing, hearing everything. I want to be hands touching, touching everything. I want to be mouth tasting, tasting everything. I want to be heart feeling, feeling everything.

I want to be life doing, doing everything.

That's all.

AFTER YOU READ

Reflect and respond

In your notebook, record three of your favourite words or phrases from the story. Give reasons for your choices.

Favourite Words	Reasons

THE FINAL GAME

Written and illustrated by William Roy Brownridge

When I was a boy growing up on the Prairies, hockey was the most important thing in my life. I had a clubfoot. My leg and foot were twisted so I couldn't wear skates. But that didn't matter. I could play goal in my moccasins, so my teammates called me Moccasin Danny.

Our hockey team was called the Wolves. I joined the team late in the season, along with my friends Petou and Anita. Petou was small but fast. Anita, who could play as well as any boy, was the first girl to join the league.

LEARNING GOALS

You will

- read a true story about an author's memories of a special hockey game
- use illustrations to predict what happens in the story

21

At first Petou, Anita, and I played well and were part of the team. But whenever we lost a game, some of the Wolves began to grumble. Travis, who was our best forward, called us "the wimps" and said we weren't good enough to play on the team. Our coach, Mr. Matteau, told Travis to stop complaining and look after his own game.

So instead of complaining, Travis ignored us. He never passed the puck to Anita or Petou in practice, not even in games.

But somehow we managed to win enough to make it to the finals against the best team in the league. The Bombers were tough and fast, and the final game would be played on their home ice.

The Bombers had a wonderful rink with new dressing rooms and grandstand seating on one side with a huge sign that said, "Home of the Bombers." This would be the biggest game ever for the Wolves. The more I thought about it, the more tense and worried I became.

One morning before the final game, the piercing hoot of the train whistle woke me with a start. I jumped out of bed and ran to the window. Over the rooftops a plume of white smoke billowed in the distance. My heart leapt. I had forgotten! My brother was on that train. Bob was a star left-winger for the Toronto Maple Leafs. He was coming home to rest an injured shoulder.

I arrived at the station late and out of breath. Coach Matteau, all the members of the Wolves, and half the town were there.

After the cheers and noisy greetings had died down, I heard the coach say, "Bob, the team has their final playoff game tomorrow. Would you come to our practice this afternoon?"

I could barely see my brother through the crowd. "Sure, coach," he said. Then he spotted me. "But first I'm going to visit my family."

The crowd moved aside and he walked toward me, whisked me up in one arm and hugged me tight. He looked like a hero in his jacket with the famous Maple Leaf crest.

That afternoon, as Bob and the coach skated out to practice, a ripple of excitement ran through the team. Everyone was thrilled to have a real pro teach us. At first, Bob worked the team through some passing and shooting drills. All the Wolves played their best. But in our practice game, Travis tried to be the star. Instead of passing to Petou, Travis attempted to stickhandle through the whole team, and was checked and lost the puck. "What a puck hog," Petou muttered.

At the end of the practice, Mr. Matteau called the team together. "You've shown Bob and me that you have the skills to win tomorrow, but the question is: Can you play as a team? Please think about that when you go home tonight."

The next afternoon, a huge crowd cheered as the two teams took to the ice. The cheering became a roar when Bob, wearing his Leaf jacket, walked to the Wolves' bench.

I crouched in goal, torn between eagerness and fear. A jumble of loud voices called out, "Come on, Wolves!" "Come on, Moccasin Danny!" and "Go Bombers, Go!"

From the opening face-off, our captain Marcel took charge and scored on a give-and-go with a sizzling shot to the goalie's glove side. Then Anita scored in a wild scramble in front of the Bombers' net. We were flying high and leading two to zero.

But in the final moments of the period, one of our defencemen tried to carry the puck out of the Wolves' zone instead of passing. He was checked and the Bombers scored on me. I looked at our bench. Bob and Coach Matteau just shook their heads.

The second period was a battle. The Bombers tried to pick on Anita, roughing and tripping her without drawing a penalty. Finally they cross-checked her to the ice. She came to the bench fighting back tears. Travis yelled out,

"What's the matter, wimp? Can't you take it?"

Somehow we held the Bombers off. By the end of the second period we still were leading two to one.

By the dying moments of the third period, we thought we had won. But the Bomber captain beat our defence and moved in on me home-free. Petou, in a desperate move, tripped him from behind, and the referee whistled a penalty shot. It would be just him and me: the Bombers' top scorer against Moccasin Danny. I felt dizzy. My opponent sneered.

He came at me from centre ice with a burst of speed and blur of stickhandling. Then he whipped a high hard shot to my glove side. I got a piece of it, but the puck dropped into the net behind me. A minute later the buzzer sounded the end of the period. The game was tied. We were going into overtime.

I left the ice, my stomach tied in knots.

The dressing room was quiet. Heads down, we tried to gather our strength. Bob stood and broke the silence. "You're playing well. Keep pressing. Coach Matteau and I just want to make one change. Travis, you join Marcel's line with Petou on the wing."

Travis grinned at Marcel. But, as usual, he ignored Petou.

"Before we go," Bob continued, "I'd like to tell you how I injured my shoulder. We were leading the New York Rangers by one goal and the game was almost over. The Rangers came on a rush and one of our defencemen fell down. I had to back-check against their fastest winger. Just as the Ranger took a pass and was about to score, I managed to lift his stick and the goal was saved. We won the game, but I crashed into the boards at top speed. I had to do whatever I could to help the Leafs. That's what you do when you play this game. You play for the team."

Bob moved behind Travis, patted his back, and whispered something in his ear. Then he looked up and said, "Now let's go get 'em!"

The Bombers came at us in waves. I fought off so many shots I started to wonder if there were two pucks instead of one.

One vicious shot glanced off my stick and rolled toward the goal line. Out of nowhere, Anita threw herself flat on the ice and hooked the puck to the corner. What a save!

We quickly counter-attacked with Marcel scooping up the puck and charging to centre ice. He passed to Travis, who broke across the blue line in full flight. Travis stick-handled furiously but two Bombers pushed him into a corner.

Travis was trapped. Wildly he looked around for another teammate, but no one was in the clear. Just as the Bombers moved in to take the puck, Travis looked over to the goal.

Little Petou, unnoticed, was alone at the open side of the Bombers' net. Quickly Travis whipped a pass across the ice.

Petou coolly tipped it in.

The game was over! We won!

The crowd cheered as Officer Adams presented the North Line cup to our captain Marcel. As the commotion began to die down, I called out, "Hey Travis, what did Bob whisper to you just before we went on the ice?"

The crowd fell silent as all eyes turned to Travis.

Travis shrugged and smiled. "He said, 'Watch for Petou. The Bombers don't cover him.'" Everyone cheered and laughed. Coach Matteau hoisted Petou on his shoulders and carried him off the ice.

We celebrated long into the night at Chong's Cafe. We didn't want the evening to end. Everyone told and retold their story of the game.

As we finally tumbled out of the cafe, Bob put his arm around Petou and led him over to Travis. "So I guess there are no wimps on this team, are there?" he said.

Travis looked at Petou and nodded. "No wimps—just winners," he answered with a grin.

AFTER YOU READ

Check your predictions

Return to your chart and record what really happens in the story in the second column. Did the illustrations help you to make predictions?

My Mama Had a Dancing Heart

Written by Libba Moore Gray
Illustrated by Raúl Colón

$\mathcal{M}$y mama had a dancing heart
and she shared that heart with me.

With a grin and a giggle,
a hug and a whistle,
we'd slap our knees
and Mama would say:
"Bless the world
it feels like
a tip-tapping
song-singing
finger-snapping
kind of day.
Let's celebrate!"
And so we did.

When a warm spring rain
would come pinging on the windowpane,
we'd kick off our shoes
and out into the rain we'd go.

We'd dance
a frog-hopping
leaf-growing
flower-opening
hello spring ballet.

High-stepping and splashing,
the rain running down our faces,
I'd slip-swish behind Mama
through the newly green grass.

And afterward
we'd read rain poems
and drink sassafras tea
with lemon curls floating.

And in summer
when the waves would come
plash-splashing on the shore,
out we'd go into the red-orange morning
with kites and balloons
tied to our wrists.

We'd do a seabird-flapping
dolphin-arching
hello summer ballet,
with me following Mama,
the sand stuck between the toes
of our up-and-down squish-squashing feet.

And afterward
we'd seashell-pile the windowsill
and drink lemonade cold.

*A*nd when the cool autumn winds
would come puff-puffing
through the clouds,
and the hold-on-tight leaves
would finally let go and float-flutter
to the ground,
out we'd go into the eye-blinking blue air,
with Mama leading in a leaf-kicking
leg-lifting
hand-clapping
hello autumn ballet.

And afterward
we'd wax paper—press leaves
red and gold
and drink hot tea spiced.

And when the winter snows
came softly down
shawling the earth,
out we'd go
and do a body-flat
arms-moving-up-and-down
snow-angel
hello winter ballet.

And then we'd stand up,
Mama first,
and dance in slow motion,
like hand-mittened
galoshes-galumphing
funny old snowmen.

And afterward
we'd cut snowflakes
paper-white delicate
and sip cocoa
with marshmallows floating.

*A*nd now
after satin-ribboning my feet
and listening to the violins
sing-swelling
around me,
onto the stage I go
air-daring
leap-flying
wing-soaring
letting the
spring rain
summer waves
autumn leaves
winter snow
carry me along until
the music slows
and I feather-float
down ... down
to the ground.

And afterward
I imagine that
I hear my mama saying:
"Bless the world
it feels like
a tip-tapping
song-singing
finger-snapping
kind of day.
Let's celebrate!"

38

*M*y mama had a dancing heart
and she shared that heart with me.

AFTER YOU READ

Note words and phrases that describe

Draw a picture of your favourite part of the story. Around the
picture, write down words and phrases the author uses to help
you "see," "feel," or "hear" the scene.

One Prairie Morning

Written by students of Briercrest School, Briercrest, Saskatchewan
Illustrated by Susan Leopold

READING TIP

Think of your experiences

Think about the things you do in the morning before you go to school. Make a list including interesting details of your morning routine.

I woke up to the sound of the tractor starting. Dad was clearing the snow from the driveway for the bus.

I rolled off my bed, yawned, and got dressed. As I entered the kitchen, Mom said, "Good morning! You'd better hurry and do your chores."

I slowly slipped into my ski pants and put on my old, bulky parka. I tugged my toque down over my head until it covered my ears and eyebrows. I put on my boots and my mitts. The only part of my body showing was my eyes. I felt like a grizzly bear.

I grabbed the bag of food scraps and headed out to the barn.

I trudged through the deep snowdrifts. Even though it was dark, I could see the hoarfrost on the trees. It reminded me of the tinsel trees in the shopping malls.

As I was looking for the biggest snow bank, something caught my eye. I thought it was a coyote, but as it came closer, I realized it was my dog. He joined me as I filled the pails with chop. When the calves saw me, they bellowed. I poured the chop into the troughs.

While the calves "pigged out" on their food, I went up to the hayloft with the scraps of food. The cats began meowing.

I accidentally stepped on one of the kittens' paws. She hissed and tried to swat my foot. I quickly threw the scraps around, making sure each cat got a piece.

I closed the barn door and latched it. As I began to run, I felt like I was on quicksand. My feet were constantly sinking through the snow. Suddenly my right foot felt cold. I looked down to see my boot stuck in the snow. I yanked it out and fell on my behind.

Once I had placed my cold boot back onto my foot, I continued my walk to the house. When I entered the house, my mom said, "You'd better hurry and eat or you'll miss the bus."

I quickly grabbed a bowl, scooped some porridge into it, and began to eat.

Suddenly I saw two lights coming down the road. "The bus!" I shouted. I quickly put on my winter clothes and boots. I grabbed my lunch, ran out the door, and hurried down the driveway.

Once I got on the bus, I began to think about the Prairies. I couldn't imagine not living on the farm.

Winter would be different. I wouldn't have a dugout to skate on or the coulees to slide down. I wouldn't be able to ski and snowmobile on the flat fields of stubble. I wouldn't have the huge drifts of snow for igloos and forts. I wouldn't even get to miss school because of blizzards.

The other seasons would be different too. I would miss the seeding and harvesting of the crops. No more riding in the truck box loaded with grain. No more planting the garden and searching for earthworms in my bare feet. No more hiding up in our tree fort by the creek.

I think there would be lots of neat things to do if I lived somewhere else, but the Prairies are the best place for me!

AFTER YOU READ

Make a comparison

Use a diagram like this to show how your morning routine is the same as or different from the boy's in the story.

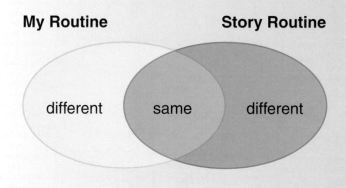

My Routine   **Story Routine**

different   same   different

JESSIE'S ISLAND

Written by Sheryl McFarlane
Illustrated by Sheena Lott

Dear Jessie,
You must be awfully bored living on an island in the middle
of nowhere. There's all kinds of things to do here, like ...
hockey, tennis, swimming, soccer, going to the zoo, video
games at the mall, eating out and then catching a movie or
a concert. And if it's cold or snowing, the planetarium or
museum are fun, and the science centre is sure to have
something new.

"I guess we'd better invite your cousin Thomas for a visit, Jessie."

Dear Thomas,
If you come to my island,
I will show you ...
the bald eagles that summer in our giant fir tree,
and the curious harbour seals that pop their
slippery, whiskered faces up when we swim to the
raft that Dad built.

And even on the greyest winter day, we can
watch for killer whales travelling up the strait,
or maybe we'll see a lone minke whale breech-feeding,
and there's a shy otter family we can see if we
paddle very quietly in the canoe.

There are so many birds to see, especially in spring ...

oyster catchers,

plovers,

sandpipers,

and gulls,

kingfishers,

coots,

mergansers,

herons,

and loons,

and harlequins so pretty, they look painted.

We'll explore the abandoned cabin where the trees grow through the roof and climb up to the point to watch the ferries pass so close it seems they could crash, except they never do.

We'll throw sticks into the swirling, frothy water just to watch them disappear or break up on the jagged rocks and peel strips of red arbutus bark until the trunk is silky smooth and we can slither down like snakes.

We'll pick huckleberries in
mid-summer

and blackberries in fall.

But my very, very favourite are
the tiny wild strawberries of early spring.

We can fish for salmon, jig for cod, dig for clams, and
set the crab trap in the bay.

We'll have fights with giant ribbons of slippery kelp,
and ...

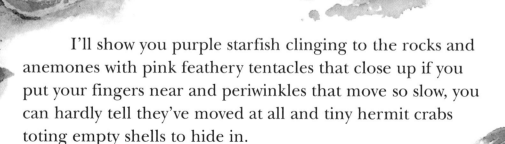

I'll show you purple starfish clinging to the rocks and
anemones with pink feathery tentacles that close up if you
put your fingers near and periwinkles that move so slow, you
can hardly tell they've moved at all and tiny hermit crabs
toting empty shells to hide in.

And when you come to visit my island, Thomas,
you might never, ever want to leave.

From your cousin,
Jessie.

AFTER YOU READ

Write a letter

Write a letter to someone you know who has not visited you
before. Tell that person what they will see if they come to visit
you. Use illustrations to explain any words they may not know.

My Name Is
Dragana

Written by Dragana Panić

Hello! My name is Dragana. I was born in one small town in Bosnia. I lived there for about seven years. When the war in Bosnia started, I moved with my family to Novi Sad in Yugoslavia. I lived there for two and one-half years.

On December 1, 1994, I came to Canada. When I came here I didn't know English. I thought I would never learn it. When I arrived, Vancouver looked pretty big to me. The first day I was sad because I was missing my best friends, cousins, and my grandmother, but I got over it.

When I started school I didn't know anybody there. When somebody said something to me I didn't understand I looked puzzled and everybody laughed at me.

I think Canada is the best country. People are polite, good and everything. In Bosnia everything is ruined and it would take a lot of time to get it ready for normal life.

I have a grandmother who is in Bosnia. She always tells me on the phone that she can't go out anywhere and that she sleeps in the bathroom. My friends don't go to school and sometimes they play inside the buildings.

Here in Canada I do everything and I think I am pretty lucky that I am here. Sometimes I still wonder why a war had to start in my country or anywhere else.

Dragana P.

AFTER YOU READ

Think about what you've learned

Write about some of the things you learned from reading about Dragana. You might want to start with these phrases:

- I learned ...
- I wonder ...
- I worry ...

AND WHO ARE YOU?

Written by Sheree Fitch
Illustrated by Dusan Petricic

My name is ...
  Alphonse Alawishes
   Abadaba
    Bertie Bingo
     Corky Coolguy
      Dippy Dingle
       Eenie Eater
        Fenton Fergus
         Georgie Ghengis
          Harry Horton
           Ian Ivy
            Jumpy Jordan
             Koola Kala
              Lucky Loonie
               Momba Mellow
                Fly-a-Kite Mike

54

Naughty Neville
Onward Orville
Peter Pickle
Quirky Quentin
Rascal Randy
RaRaRa Raccoon!
Sweetie Sugar
Sisboombah
Twirly Tuba
Tony
Understumble Underwort
Victor Voickle Valentine
Wrinkled Willywhoops
Xylophonist Xaxafrax
Yikes the Yingy Yang
Zat's all

You might think it
A strange name
You might think it long
But you know what?
It's my name
Every name is a song

And who, may I ask, are you?

Our Arctic Home on the Web

From the web site of Leo Ussak Elementary School, Rankin Inlet, Northwest Territories

The Internet site of Leo Ussak Elementary School in Rankin Inlet, Northwest Territories, is an amazing place. This web site was created by William Belsey, Leo Ussak School's Computer Program Coordinator. The school calls itself the "coolest" school in Canada's Arctic.

Their web site has won many awards and has been visited by people from around the world. At the site, students tell about themselves on their personal web pages. You'll also learn about their Arctic home. Moving across the bottom of Leo Ussak's home page is the message *Ulakut* (oo-la-koot), which means "Good day!" in the Inuktitut language. At the end of the message is *Tagvavutit* (tug-va-voo-teet): "Until we meet again."

READING TIP

Ask questions

In this selection, students from Rankin Inlet tell about themselves on their personal web pages. Record any questions you have about where they live or about making a web page.

Rankin Inlet Community Access Centre
ᐃᒡᓚᒃᑯᑦ / Igalaaq

ᓚᐅ ᐅᔅᓴᒃ ᐃᓕᓐᓂᐊᕐᕕᒃ
LEO USSAK
ELEMENTARY SCHOOL

LEARNING GOALS

You will

- meet other students by reading their web pages

- ask questions to help you find out more about others

The World Wide Web

The World Wide Web is part of the Internet—the **Int**ernational **Net**work that links computers. At each place or *site* on the web, you see a page of text and pictures on the computer screen.

By clicking on words that are highlighted and underlined, the web automatically **links** your computer to another page on the Internet. To see web pages and follow their links, you can use a program called a *web browser*.

The first page of a web site is the place where you begin. It is called the *home page*. A home page has links that you can use to visit other pages on the site or to go to pages on different web sites.

Living in the North

Written by Nina Schweder

At the web site, student Nina Schweder tells us about where she and her school friends live.

Hi! My name is Nina Schweder and I am 11 years old. I go to Leo Ussak Elementary School. I live in Rankin Inlet. Rankin is a small town of about 2300 people and there is a lot of snow here. When we want to see the whole town, we can go up on a hill and see the Inukshuk. It looks like a human, but it is made out of rocks. In our school there are pictures of elders on the walls. Elders are very important to us. The Leo Ussak School is named after an elder from our community.

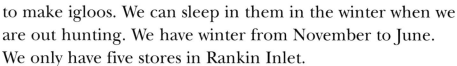

The weather in Rankin Inlet is usually very cold in winter. Sometimes we get storm days and we get snow piled up near our school, our houses, and on the road. Everyone lives in modern houses now, but the elders teach us how to make igloos. We can sleep in them in the winter when we are out hunting. We have winter from November to June. We only have five stores in Rankin Inlet.

We have a new kids' drop-in centre. We can do anything there. We can play table tennis. We have sports. Soccer and hockey are the most popular sports. In winter we play sports inside, but we go skating outside on Williamson Lake when the ice is strong enough in the fall. We have square dances at our community hall. We have them from nine until one-thirty or two in the morning. We have different tournaments in the high school gym and at the arena. We play indoor soccer, hockey, basketball, volleyball, and Inuit games. We have a pool that is open from June until September. Almost everyone in town goes swimming there.

We used to be called Eskimos, but now we are called Inuit, which means "people" in our language, Inuktitut. People say that Rankin Inlet is going to get bigger in the future, but I think Rankin should stay the way it is. It is more fun when Rankin is small. I like living in Rankin Inlet. I've been here since I was born.

NUNAVUT

Rankin Inlet
Ka-ner-thlee-niq
ᑲᖏᕐᖠᓂᖅ

On April 1, 1999, Canada as we know it will change forever. The eastern half of the Northwest Territories will become a new self-governing territory. It will be called *Nunavut* (noo-na-voot), an Inuktitut word that means "our land."

About My Web Page

Interview with Joanne Kent

We sent Joanne an e-mail letter asking her to tell about how she created her web page. She answered by e-mail.

Joanne, how did you learn to create a web page?

I learned to create a web page from my computer teacher, Mr. Bill Belsey.

What are some of the most important features on your web page?

Some of the most important features on my web page are my links, like the ones to the Montreal Canadiens and to Alanis Morissette. I chose my links because they're things I enjoy.

How did you decide what information to put on your page?

I decided to put things in about the North, because people are pretty interested in learning about it.

Do you communicate with other people through the Internet?

Yes, I do communicate with people through my web page. They've sent me e-mail. I communicate with my friends, and all the mail I've got is from Canada.

Do you plan on changing your page? If so, how?

Yes, I do plan on changing my web page by putting more links and writing more.

What does your web page tell us about you?

It tells you about what things I like, what I like doing, and what things I enjoy.

What advice would you give other kids about creating their own web pages?

You should make lots of links. Tell people about where you live. Tell people about yourself, and put things on your web page that you think are interesting. Add a graphic like a photo or a picture.

Here is Joanne's Internet web page. As you can see, she has lots of links (in blue, underlined print) to other web pages at the Leo Ussak School site and elsewhere on the Internet.

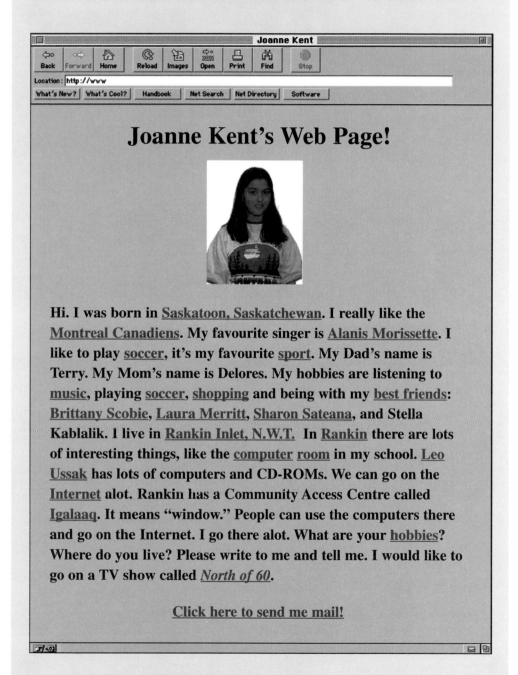

Here are some more web pages from the students of
Leo Ussak School.

Adam Tanuyak's Web Page!

Hi. My name is Adam Tanuyak. I was born in <u>Winnipeg, Manitoba</u> in 1985. I am 11 years old. I live in Rankin Inlet. I go to Leo Ussak School. My hobbies are playing street <u>hockey</u>, playing <u>chess</u>, and using our computer. I like working with computers and hope to be a <u>computer</u> programmer, but I don't know what kind of computer programmer. I like travelling. My favourite sport is <u>soccer</u>. I like watching the <u>WCW Nitro</u> a lot. I like listening to music such as <u>Oasis</u> and I like to dance. My favourite hockey teams are 50% <u>Toronto Maple Leafs</u> and 50% <u>Montreal Canadiens</u>. My favourite goalie in hockey is <u>Jocelyn Thibault</u>. I like to make designs on my computer and on a piece of paper. My design on a piece of paper is at the top of my web page.

Why the Internet Is So Important to Me

Why? Because it helps us see the outside world. It helps us find information about what we would like to learn about. It helps people understand things such as "What is a polar bear?" and it will tell you what kind of animal it is. It's like a huge encyclopedia but you use a computer and the world wide web. It lets us keep in touch with friends around the world by "chatting" and sending e-mail. I like the Internet because it keeps you busy exploring other neat web pages. This is why the Internet is so important to me.

<u>**Click here to send me mail!**</u>

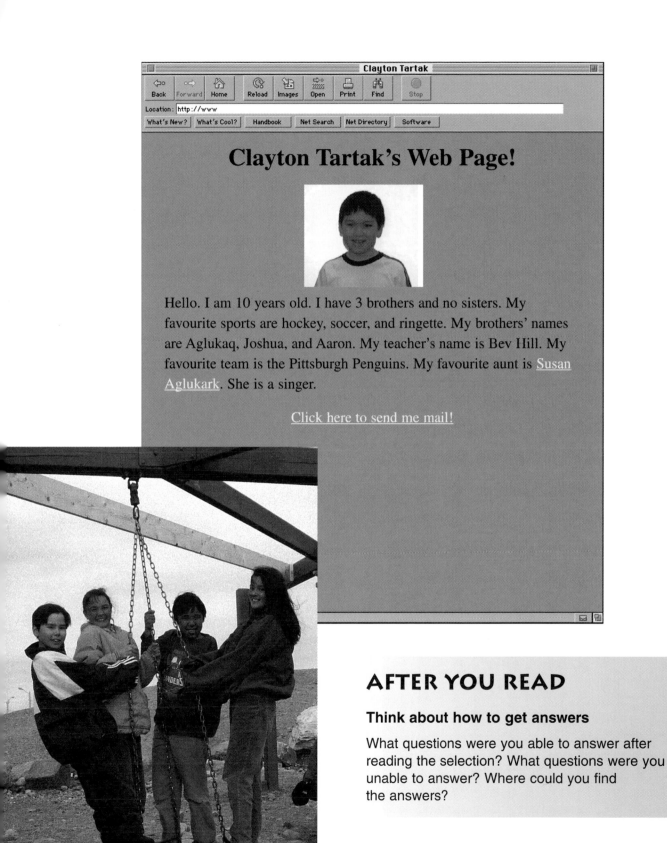

Clayton Tartak's Web Page!

Hello. I am 10 years old. I have 3 brothers and no sisters. My favourite sports are hockey, soccer, and ringette. My brothers' names are Aglukaq, Joshua, and Aaron. My teacher's name is Bev Hill. My favourite team is the Pittsburgh Penguins. My favourite aunt is Susan Aglukark. She is a singer.

Click here to send me mail!

AFTER YOU READ

Think about how to get answers

What questions were you able to answer after reading the selection? What questions were you unable to answer? Where could you find the answers?

WE ARE ALL RELATED

Written and illustrated by students of G. T. Cunningham Elementary School, Vancouver, British Columbia

George Littlechild is a Plains Cree artist who tells stories about his ancestors through his collages. When students at G. T. Cunningham Elementary School saw his paintings and collage in his book This Land Is My Land, *they were inspired to tell about their own families through art. They asked their parents and grandparents questions, and collected pictures and family photographs. Finally, they published a book. Here is an excerpt.*

READING TIP

Get information from pictures

Photos and drawings give you information that helps you understand a person and that person's feelings. Look carefully at the illustrations and the words.

LEARNING GOALS

You will

- find out how students in one school told stories about their families
- use clues to get information from pictures

I AM NAVEEN ARNEJA

My family comes from India. The elders in my collage are my grandma, grandpa, and dad. The photograph of me shows me with my grandma when I was about three years old.

I drew a sky, fence, and two religious dolls because they show strength. The border on my collage is a pattern of four lines, triangles, and fish.

I think this project was worthwhile because I learned more about my culture and family.

THE ELDERS SPEAK

"I would like young people to learn from me ... to respect the family and not to go bad."

—Prem Arneja (Naveen's grandma)

To me, "We Are All Related" means that we are all connected. Although we all look different, we are all human and we are all related. Hold on to your dream.

ਮੇਰੇ ਲਈ "ਅਸੀਂ ਸਭ ਸਬੰਧੀ ਹਾਂ" ਦਾ ਅਰਥ ਹੈ ਕਿ ਅਸੀਂ ਸਭ ਆਪਸ ਵਿਚ ਜੁੜੇ ਹੋਏ ਹਾਂ। ਦੇਖਣ ਵਿਚ ਭਾਵੇਂ ਵੱਖਰੇ ਲਗਦੇ ਹਾਂ ਪਰ ਅਸੀਂ ਸਭ ਇਨਸਾਨ ਹਾਂ ਅਤੇ ਇਕ ਦੂਜੇ ਨਾਲ ਸਬੰਧਿਤ ਹਾਂ।

I AM ERIC PETER CHO

My family comes from China and Hong Kong. The elders in this collage are my mom, Wai Fong, and my dad, Li Cho. The photograph shows me with my dad and mom. In the left corner of the picture is my mom with a purple collar. In the right corner are my mom and dad carrying me in Queen Elizabeth Park.

The border on my collage is a pattern of Chinese writing: sun, water, up and down. I drew a dragon and a tiger because they symbolize power, strength, and Chinese culture. The Chinese writing means tiger and cat.

I think this project was important because it showed our feelings and how great our art came out.

THE ELDERS SPEAK

"I would like young people to learn from me ... to find a job to do and not be bad."

—Lui An (Eric's grandpa)

To me, "We Are All Related" means that we are all connected.
Do your best and be helpful to each other and you will succeed
in the future.

我解釋「本是同根生」的定義是：我們本來都有連繫。
凡事盡力而為，彼此幫助，必定成功在望。

I AM DAVID PARENTE

My family comes from Italy. The elders in this collage are my mom, grandma, and grandpa. The photograph shows me with my mom and brother.

I drew a temple and snakes because they stand for Rome, Italy. The border on my collage is a pattern of potato prints that symbolize stars.

I think this project was neat because the project made me feel good.

THE ELDERS SPEAK

"I would like young people to learn from me ... to make their bed and not to talk back to others."
—Ledina Dinofrio (David's grandma)

70

To me, "We Are All Related" means that we are all connected.
Don't be bad and don't be a racist.

Per me, siamo tutti una grande famiglia: ciò significa che tutti
abbiamo qualcosa in comune. Non essere malvagio.
Non essere razzista.

I AM CHRISTINE WHITE

My family comes from the Philippines and Vancouver. The elders in this collage are my two grandmothers, Eva and Adela, and my grandfather. The photograph shows me when I was four years old, talking to my grandmother, Eva.

I drew a picture of a chain because it stands for peace, justice, and friendship. The border on my collage is a pattern of evergreen trees and stripes.

I think this project was outstanding because it was exciting being able to go to the gallery to see George Littlechild.

THE ELDERS SPEAK

"I would like young people to learn from me ... to learn how to behave and not to disobey their parents."
—Rose White (Christine's mom)

To me, "We Are All Related" means that we have to take care of the animals. We all have to take care, don't be greedy and be nice to other people.

Para sa akin "lahat tayo ay magkakaugnay" ay nangangahulugan na kailangan nating alagaan ang mga hayop. Lahat tayo ay dapat na maging maingat. Huwag maging sakim at maging mabuti sa pakikitungo sa kapwa.

AFTER YOU READ

Draw conclusions

Choose one person you got to know in this selection. What did the words tell you about him or her? What did the illustrations tell you?

AND WHO ARE YOU?

In this unit, you have learned about the lives of a variety of real people and story characters. Now it is *your* turn to tell others about *you* by making a collection of your work.

BEFORE YOU BEGIN

Think and talk about what your collection will look like. Ask yourself these questions:

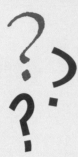

- Who will read and look at my work?
- What do I want people to know about me?
- What kinds of work will tell others about me?
- How will I put my collection together?

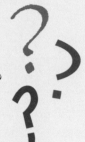

Why not plan your collection using a web?
Here is the web that Matthew used.

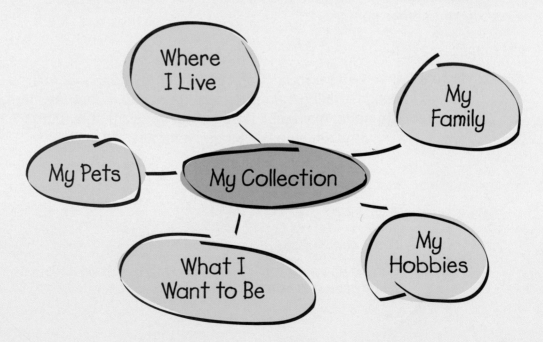

YOUR FIRST DRAFT

1. Choose Your Most Interesting Work

- Read and view each piece of work. Think about ways you can improve it.

- Think about your learning, using the questions on page 77.

- Make a new copy of any pieces you decide to change.

Looking Back at Your Work

- a story about someone special in your life
- a friendly letter
- a poem about what you can do
- a list of things you'd like to be
- a collage about your family

Remember to find an interesting way to start your introduction. You want to "hook" your reader.

2. Write Information About Yourself

- What else would you like your readers to know about you?

- Look back at your planning web or chart for some ideas.

- Write your introduction.

Here is an example of Sam's introduction.

Sam Mcleod's Web Page!!

Hi, I'm Sam. I have lived in Rankin Inlet all my life. It's okay, I guess, but I like Winnipeg better. I like to play soccer and hockey. I guess I'm pretty much an Inuk. I can hardly talk Inuktituk but I'm starting to learn. My favourite colours are green and black. I enjoy string braiding and writing to my cousin in Winnipeg on the Internet. My best friends are Catherine and Susanne. They both are from Coral Harbour. My teacher's name is Margaret. My computer teacher's name is Bill. He is the best computer teacher ever. My teacher said I can be a grade one teacher. I want to learn the bagpipes—they are really loud!

3. Put It All Together

Decide how you will put all the pieces of your collection together.

Here is Krystal Katie's collection of work. She decided to make a poster.

I am Krystal Katie. I live in Stoney Creek, Ontario, and go to Green Acres School. I hate my name because it sounds like two peoples' names. I also dislike rainy days. I like to sing in the shower. My family thinks it's really funny. My favourite things to do are drawing and watching figure skating.

My Brother Has an Energetic Life

My brother has an energetic life and he shares it all with me.
In the time of spring
my brother and I:
football-playing
grass-stomping
feet-falling.
It is that kind of day.

My Collection

I Want to Be …

- I want to be smart, but not so smart that I can't get anything wrong.
- I want to be popular, but not so popular that I can't remember the names of all my friends.
- I want to be purple, but not so purple that I look like a grape.

Dear Kalpna,

If you come to Stoney Creek you will meet a lot of people. You can go for hikes—that's fun! Or you can go tobogganing at Battlefield Park. There's a lot of people there! Oh and there's lots of candy stores. The most fun of all are fairs. They are fun because there's lots of rides and games. If you come I would take you to my trailer and you can swim there. There are lots of places to fish. You would have lots of fun at my trailer with all those things to do! So hope you would like it!

Sincerely your friend,
Krystal Katie McMaster

REVISE AND EDIT

Go back and review what you have included in your collection that tells about you.

- Ask a classmate or friend to look at your work. Listen to their suggestions. Are there ways to improve what you've done?

- Proofread your work for errors in spelling, punctuation, and grammar.

- Have you used complete sentences? capital letters for names and sentence beginnings? periods or question marks at the end of sentences or questions?

Ways to Share Your Collection

- the Internet
- a scrapbook
- a bulletin-board display
- a read-aloud and viewing presentation
- a computer printout

Think About Your Learning

Add your own ideas about what makes a good collection of work.

- Does each piece tell something about me?
- Have I included different forms of writing to make it interesting for the audience?
- Are there details that I could add?
- Are there parts that are unclear and hard to understand?
- Is the way I put it all together interesting and easy for others to follow?

Unit 2: *Explore and Observe*

In this unit you will begin to see the world around you as a scientist does. You will observe different environments and will explore them from the points of view of the observed and the observer. Using the tools of observation, you will be asked to take notes, make diagrams, discuss what you think is happening, and use what you know about the world to develop new understandings of everyday events. You will

- read a wide variety of materials, such as diagrams, poetry, an interview, and a story
- learn how to get information from your reading and viewing
- learn how to record and to present information
- write an observation report

Ways We Observe

Written by Maureen Skinner

We observe with our eyes…

…the beauty of
a delicate leaf…

…the hidden world of
the small and unseen…

… the images we create
with our hands…

… how the cycle of nature changes…

… how much of life is similar…

… in our incredible world.

BEACH

Written by Lilian Moore

STONES

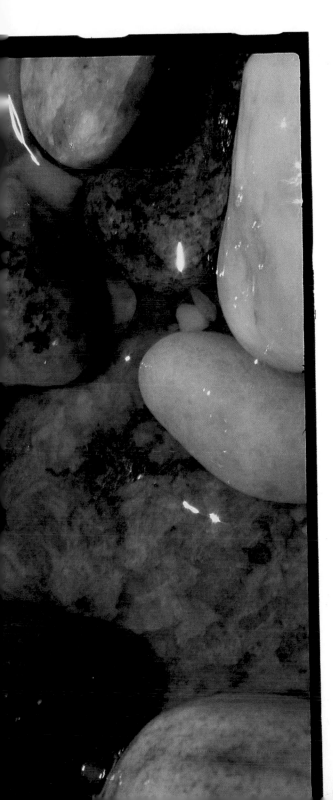

When these small
stones
were
in clear pools and
nets of weed

tide-tumbled
teased by spray

they glowed
moonsilver,
glinted sunsparks on
their speckled
skins.

Spilled on the
shelf
they were
wet-sand jewels
wave-green
still flecked with
foam.

Now
gray stones
lie
dry and dim.

Why did we bring them home?

Ocean Tides & Tidepools

Written by Adrienne Mason
Illustrated by Bernadette Lau and Johnny Wú

Tides are the daily rise and fall of the world's oceans. If you've been to the beach you might have noticed that the water creeps up the beach (high tide), then back down (low tide) throughout the day. The constant pull of the moon's and sun's gravity are the main tide makers. The effect of the moon's pull is the greatest. That's because, even though the moon is smaller than the sun, it is much closer to our Earth. The sun and moon are not strong enough to pull the Earth out of shape. But they do pull at the oceans. The oceans bulge, and this bulge creates tides.

LEARNING GOALS

You will

- find out about tides and tidepools
- find information to answer questions
- make a plan to collect information

Life on the Rocks

Pretend that you are a tiny sea creature living on a rocky shore, where the land and sea meet. This *intertidal zone* is covered with water during high tides and in the open air during low tides. It can be a pretty tough place to live.

During low tide you are exposed to the air, wind, sun, rain, and snow. The hot sunlight makes your temperature rise. The wind dries you out. Hungry seagulls, raccoons, and other predators try to eat you.

Life isn't much easier when the tide starts coming in. The first wave of the rising tide hits you and your temperature drops. Wave after wave pounds over you, almost pulling you off the rocks. Predators from the sea begin to hunt—you!

Creatures that live in the intertidal zone are well adapted to their changing environment. Some, such as the tiny periwinkle, are almost land creatures. They can survive with only a splash of water every so often. Others are very much sea creatures. They can stand being in the open air only briefly.

In many places the intertidal zone is divided into bands called *subzones*. Each subzone has a different grouping of plants and animals that can adapt to each area. Competition is tough for both space and food, and those that can't compete must live higher up in the intertidal zone.

Predators have a major influence on where creatures live. For example, you won't see many mussels in the area where sea stars live. Mussels are sea stars' favourite food! As you go higher up in the intertidal zone, conditions are too hard for sea stars to survive. Above this point, mussels can live without danger of being eaten.

The Mid-tide Zone

There are more creatures here, and many different kinds. Plants and animals spend hours at a time either underwater or exposed to the air, as the tide covers and uncovers them once or twice a day.

The Low-tide Zone

This zone is almost always underwater and is only exposed during very low tides. Conditions change less often than in the zones above, and the animals here are less adapted to living in the open air. Many kinds of seaweed grow in the low-tide zone, providing homes and food for many animals.

Tidepools

Water collects in cracks and hollows, creating pools like this one. Tidepool creatures are always covered by seawater, so they don't dry out. But rain can quickly make the pool less salty, and the sun can overheat the water. Low tide is a great time to explore tidepools.

The Spray Zone

This area gets only splashes from waves— unless there is a storm. Few plants and animals live here. They are more creatures of the land than the sea.

The High-tide Zone

Here, plants and animals are covered with water during the highest tides, but are left high and dry during low tides. The creatures living here, and in the other zones below, are experts at hanging on. Waves crash and break over them with violent force. Barnacles are common here.

Nature's Aquariums: Tidepools

Look into a tidepool and you'll see many amazing creatures.

Hermit Crabs don't have a hard outer shell to protect them like most crabs, so they have to borrow one. This hermit crab has taken over an empty shell, which it uses as a mobile home. It will move into a bigger shell as it grows.

To a *Sculpin* there's no place like home. If it is washed out of its tidepool, a homing instinct helps it find its way back. Because of their colouring and small size, sculpins are often hard to spot—unless they are hungry. Then they become very lively, gripping onto food and spinning around until a chunk tears off.

Tube Worms, "cousins" of earthworms, build strong tubes of calcium or sand to live in. They stick out their long tentacles to eat and breathe. When in danger, they pull back into their tubes.

The *Sea Cucumber* wedges its squishy body into cracks and under rocks—perfect hiding places from hungry predators. Its sticky tentacles wave in the water and collect food that floats by. Then the sea cucumber puts a tentacle into its mouth and "licks" it clean.

Be a Tidepool Explorer

To get a better look at life in a tidepool—or in shallow water—make a waterscope.

Seashore Safety

Follow these guidelines when exploring the home of intertidal creatures—for their safety and yours.

- Never turn your back on the waves. Large waves can come up suddenly, sweeping people off the rocks.
- Observe the animals where you find them. It is very difficult to keep sea creatures alive away from the beach.
- Always return animals and plants to the place you found them.
- Always fill any holes you make in the sand.
- Do not forcibly pry off animals and plants that are attached to rock.

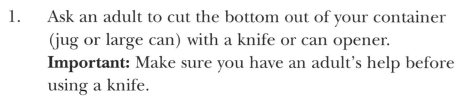

You'll need:

- a plastic jug or large tin can
- a knife or can opener
- scissors
- plastic wrap
- an elastic band or piece of elastic
- black plastic electrical tape or other waterproof tape

1. Ask an adult to cut the bottom out of your container (jug or large can) with a knife or can opener. **Important:** Make sure you have an adult's help before using a knife.
2. Cut a piece of plastic wrap large enough to cover the bottom of your container.
3. Secure the plastic wrap with an elastic band or piece of elastic. Make sure the elastic is tight.
4. Tape down the edges of the plastic wrap with the waterproof tape.
5. Try out your waterscope. Put the plastic-wrapped end in the water and look through the open end.

AFTER YOU READ

Find answers

Look back at the questions in the chart you made. Cross out any that were answered in the article, and add any new ones you have. Add a new column called "How I could find answers" and jot down your ideas.

Visit Niagara Parks Butterfly Conservatory

Written by Todd Mercer

READING TIP

Think like an author

Pretend you are writing about an interesting place. How could you make your readers feel like they were there? As you read, think about how this author does it.

Imagine a building where live butterflies float by you in a jungle atmosphere. From time to time, the brilliantly coloured creatures land on your shoulder or on tropical plants to feed.

This very real building is in Canada! It's called the Niagara Parks Butterfly Conservatory, home to North America's largest collection of free-flying butterflies.

The Conservatory is a great place to practise your observation skills. There are around 2000 live butterflies to look at. They include 70 of the 24 000 species in the world.

The first stop on this Conservatory tour is a small theatre where you'll watch a video about butterflies. Here you'll learn interesting facts about the insects. Did you know that they feel, hear, and smell with their antennae, and taste with their feet?

You'll also learn that butterflies are very delicate creatures. It's important not to disturb them or their environment because they can die easily. So there are important rules to follow when you enter the display area, such as not touching the butterflies and collecting only butterfly pictures with a camera, not real butterflies.

The fun starts when you enter the huge glass building that houses the plants and butterflies. First you'll probably notice butterflies fluttering all around in jungle-like heat. And, *hisssssss*. What's that? A poisonous snake? No, it's one of the nozzles spraying mist to keep the air humid—just like the air in a tropical rain forest.

93

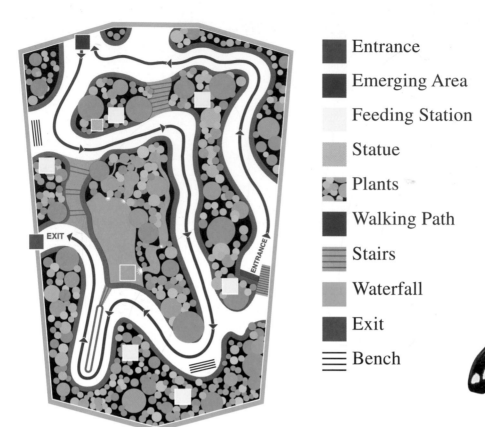

Entrance

Emerging Area

Feeding Station

Statue

Plants

Walking Path

Stairs

Waterfall

Exit

Bench

EXIT

ENTRANCE

Your walking tour begins at the foot of a stone pathway that's 180 m long. The trail climbs and weaves past a human-made waterfall and stream. On each side of the pathway are an amazing number of plants from many areas of the world such as Brazil, Polynesia, Japan, China, Australia, India, and Fiji. Some of these plants provide food for butterflies.

But wait! What's that over there on a stone soaking up sunlight? Maybe some alien space creature? No, it's two of the four green iguanas that are in the Conservatory to add to the jungle atmosphere.

Of course, the main attraction is the butterflies. There are brilliant blue butterflies, bright orange ones, yellow ones, brown spotted ones, black-and-white spotted ones, pink spotted ones, and butterflies with many other colours and markings.

Some butterflies are difficult to spot because they blend in with their natural surroundings. Others, with their brilliant colours, are hard to miss. Many of the most colourful butterflies are poisonous to other jungle creatures. Their bright colours are Nature's way of warning birds and animals that SWALLOWING THESE BUTTERFLIES COULD BE DANGEROUS TO YOUR HEALTH. In this way, the bright colours allow butterflies to protect themselves from harm.

With all you've seen on your Conservatory tour, it would be great to talk to an expert and learn more about butterflies.

AFTER YOU READ

Discuss writing strategies

How did Todd Mercer make you feel like you were at the Butterfly Conservatory? Work with two or three friends to talk about your ideas.

Meet a Butterfly Expert

Written by Todd Mercer

LEARNING GOALS

You will

- read an interview
- note what makes a good interview question

READING TIP

Read interviews

In an interview, the questions are just as important as the answers. Reading the questions carefully will help you understand the answers.

As curator of the Niagara Parks Butterfly Conservatory, Mel Dell manages the building, orders butterflies from breeders all over the world, and helps educate visitors about these beautiful insects.

Mel's job allows him to combine his love of science and nature. He's also an *entomologist*, a scientist who specializes in studying insects.

He talked with me about the Conservatory's fabulous butterfly collection and provided some valuable tips on observing live butterflies in the jungle-like display.

How is the Conservatory specially suited to butterflies?

Our glass roof is very high. It's 20 m from the floor to the peak of the roof, and the building is wide and long. The large area is similar to the open environment where butterflies live in nature. As a result, you can see butterflies behaving as they would in the wild.

These butterflies come to us from all over the world. So sections of the Conservatory are designed to look and feel like these different world areas, with the plants that naturally grow there. Some types of butterflies enjoy shady areas. Others, like the Morpho and Owl butterflies, prefer to soar up to great heights.

Blue Morpho

Magnificent Owl

Butterflies must be delicate creatures.

They are. So their conservatory environment has to be carefully controlled. Computers make sure the humidity, or the amount of water in the air, is just right. The air in the building is circulated at low speeds because we don't want the butterflies blown around. And the parking lot is located far away from the Conservatory. Small traces of harmful car gases could kill butterflies.

How long do butterflies usually live?

It varies quite a lot. The more delicate species don't last much more than seven to ten days. Most of them last about two weeks. The Blue Morpho and the Owl butterflies usually last about three weeks. In some cases, the Longwing butterflies from Central America can last a month or more if they're given the proper food.

How do you keep the Conservatory filled with butterflies?

We need to bring in about 4000 butterflies a month to maintain our display of around 2000 butterflies at any one time. Many of the butterflies come to us regularly from suppliers in Costa Rica, El Salvador, the Philippines, Malaysia, and Florida. As well, we raise some Longwing butterflies in the Conservatory. We need to raise about 400 to 500 butterflies per week to keep up with our high turnover of butterflies.

Can you actually see the butterflies being raised in the Conservatory?

The butterflies we're raising are in a separate area. But when the butterflies arrive from other parts of the world, they're in the chrysalis stage. We hang the chrysalises on racks in the Emerging Area, which is covered with clear plastic. Visitors can actually see new butterflies hatching.

A butterfly grows through four stages in its life. This change is called *metamorphosis*.

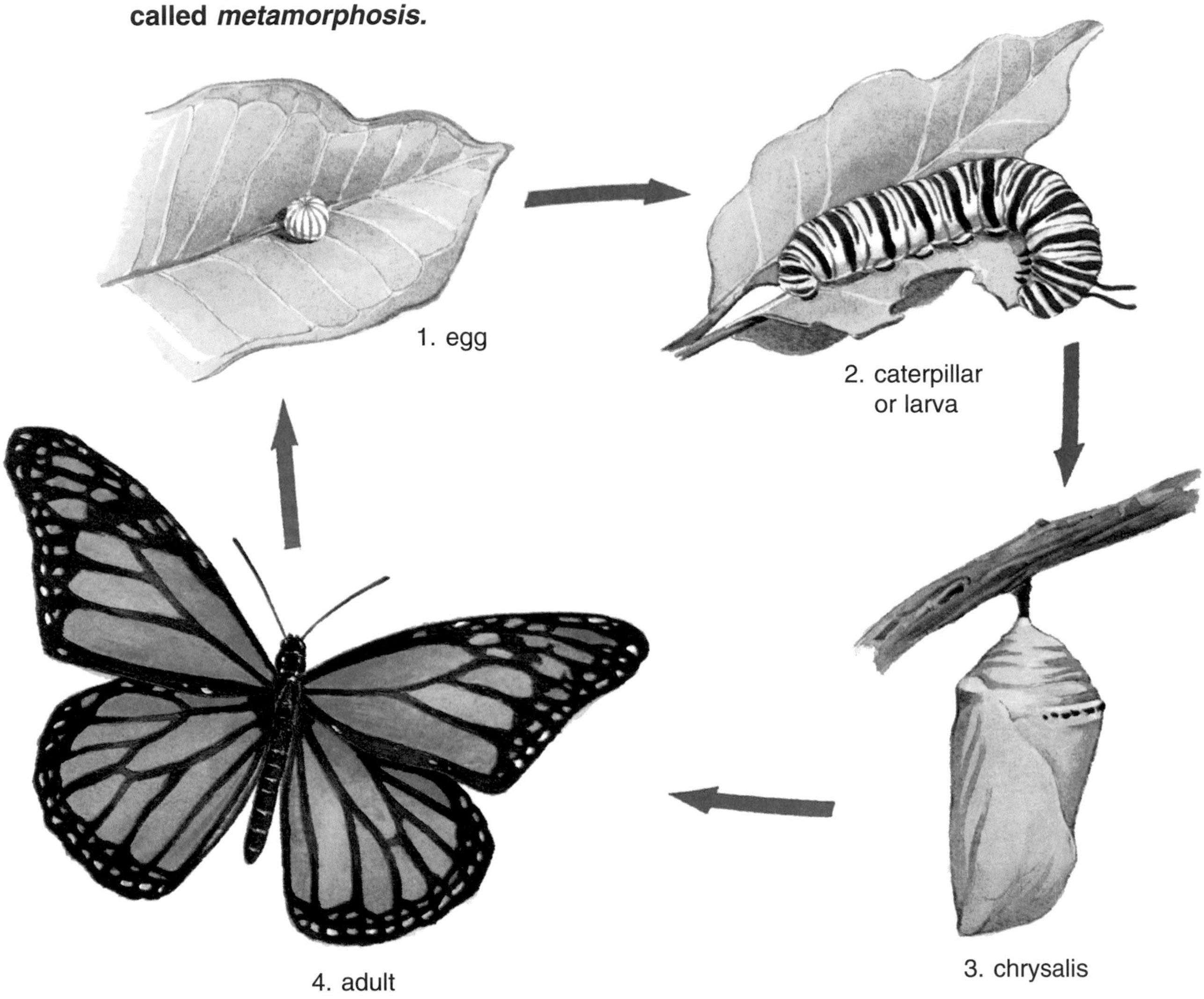

1. egg

2. caterpillar or larva

3. chrysalis

4. adult

What interesting things should visitors look for when observing butterflies?

They might start by observing and comparing butterfly shapes. Although the insects may have different colours, some butterflies are related because their wings share a common shape.

Tiger Longwing

Zebra Longwing

Then, there's butterfly size. We have a full range of sizes from very tiny butterflies, right up to the Giant Owl butterfly. Our biggest house guest is the Atlas moth, which is about 20 to 25 cm across.

Visitors might look at butterflies' flight habits. Some have darting movements. Others seem to leisurely float through the Conservatory.

Or you could look at their behaviour. The Morpho butterflies often fly through the vegetation in groups of five or six. They follow each other in single file.

It's also interesting to compare butterflies' feeding habits. Some butterflies feed on the nectar from plants and others obtain their food from the liquid on ripe fruit.

What observation tools do you use at the Conservatory?

The scientific staff use microscopes and hand lenses to scout for pest problems on the exhibits. Some of these pests can be very tiny insects such as spider mites.

We've noticed on cloudy days that many butterflies hang around on the netting up near the roof. Some of our visitors have observed this pattern, and on return visits, they bring along binoculars to have a better look.

Butterflies Close Up

A butterfly's tongue is called a *proboscis*. It's hollow, like a drinking straw. The butterfly uses it to drink nectar from flowers. A butterfly's mouth is constructed so it can only handle liquids.

Butterfly blood is not red like people's blood. It can be brown, yellow, or green.

Butterflies have compound eyes. Compound eyes have many flat sides, called *facets*. Each facet sees a separate picture. This allows butterflies to see movement quite well.

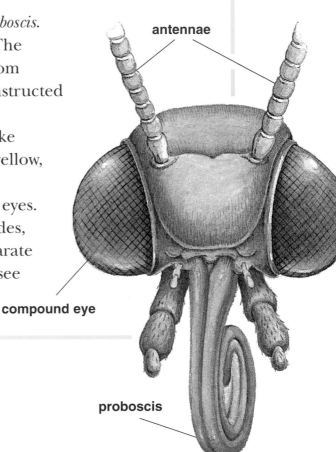

antennae

compound eye

proboscis

AFTER YOU READ

Write interview questions

Take another look at the questions Todd Mercer asked. What makes a good interview question? Write two good questions you would like to add to this interview.

The Cabbage White Butterfly

Written by Elizabeth Jennings

I look like a flower you could pick. My delicate wings
Flutter over the cabbages. I don't make
Any noise ever. I'm among silent things.
Also I easily break.

I have seen the nets in your hands. At first I thought
A cloud had come down but then I noticed you
With your large pink hand and arm. I was nearly caught
But fortunately I flew

Away in time, hid while you searched, then took
To the sky, was out of your reach. Like a nameless flower
I tried to appear. Can't you be happy to look?
Must you possess with your power?

BEEHIVE ALIVE

Written by Laura Edlund
Illustrated by Jack McMaster

Imagine it's a warm sunny day, with bees buzzing and a light breeze carrying the scent of flowers. One bee flies to a tree trunk and suddenly seems to disappear. The bee is returning to its hive with nectar and flower pollen.

Hive Inside Hollow Tree Trunk

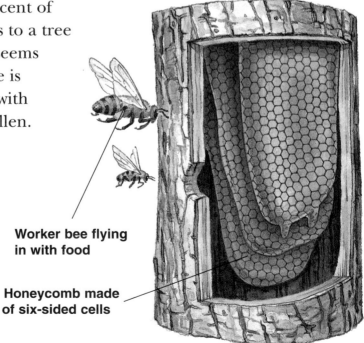

Worker bee flying in with food

Honeycomb made of six-sided cells

Worker bee collecting pollen and nectar

21 Days of Bee Development

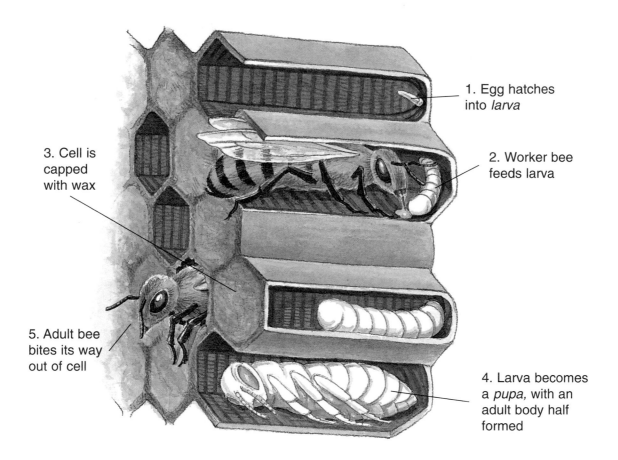

1. Egg hatches into *larva*

2. Worker bee feeds larva

3. Cell is capped with wax

4. Larva becomes a *pupa*, with an adult body half formed

5. Adult bee bites its way out of cell

A hive is a community of thousands of bees living and working inside honeycombs. Honeycombs are made from wax that bees make in their bodies. Bees make honey and store it for the winter, lay eggs, and raise infant bees in the hive.

LEARNING GOALS

You will

- read diagrams and text
- compare ways to read information

Three ranks of bees live in the hive. Each kind of bee has its special job.

Drones

The drones are male and have one job—to mate with the queen. Drones are born in the spring. At the end of the summer, they are taken from the hive and left to die.

Workers

Worker bees gather nectar and pollen, make honey and wax, build the honeycomb, look after the queen and infants, and guard the hive. Most bees are worker bees. They are female and they live for about five weeks.

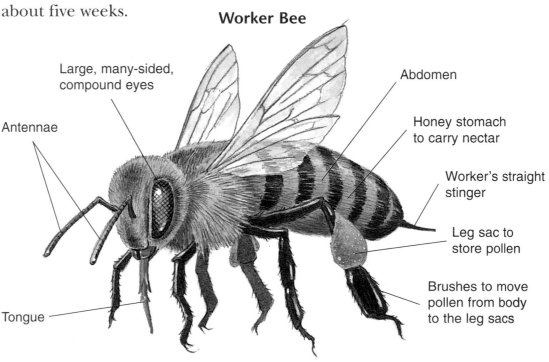

Worker cells, about 5 mm across

Worker bees "dancing" to tell other workers where to find good food

Pollen stored in cells

Larvae developing in cells

Honey stored in cells

Worker Bee

Large, many-sided, compound eyes

Antennae

Tongue

Abdomen

Honey stomach to carry nectar

Worker's straight stinger

Leg sac to store pollen

Brushes to move pollen from body to the leg sacs

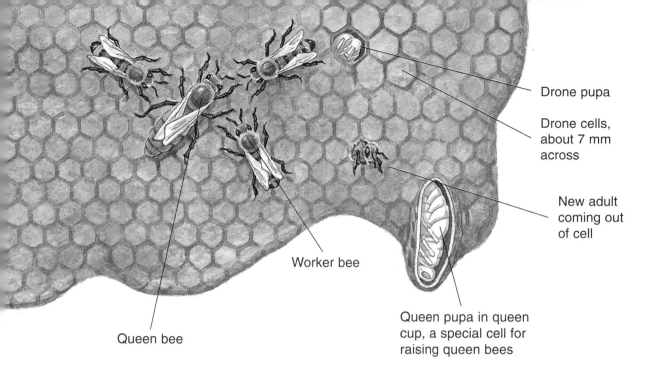

Drone pupa

Drone cells, about 7 mm across

New adult coming out of cell

Queen pupa in queen cup, a special cell for raising queen bees

Worker bee

Queen bee

The Queen

The queen mates, lays eggs, and keeps order in the hive. She lives for about three years. After she mates with the drones, she spends her time laying eggs—up to 2000 a day!

The queen produces an oily substance with a strong scent. When the workers clean her, they lick off the substance and share it around. The substance controls the workers' behaviour and makes them stick to their jobs.

When the queen gets old, she lays some eggs in queen cups. The first of these bees to hatch uses her long curved stinger to kill the queens still in their queen cups. If two hatch at the same time, they fight. Whichever survives becomes the new queen. Meanwhile, worker bees stop feeding the old queen so that she dies.

The queen also lays eggs in queen cups when her hive becomes overcrowded. Then she and some worker bees fly off to build a new hive.

AFTER YOU READ

Compare diagrams and text

Did you get more information from the diagrams or the text? Give your reasons.

LADYBUG GARDEN

Written and illustrated by Celia Godkin

The gardener looked all around his garden, and he liked what he saw. There were hardy vegetables, brightly coloured flowers, and fruit trees that made the air smell sweet. There were many kinds of insects in the garden, too: ladybugs and wasps, bees and butterflies, aphids and ants.

The gardener thought about all those insects. He knew that bees and butterflies helped the garden grow. As they flew from flower to flower, drinking nectar, they picked up a fine yellow dust called pollen, which the flowers produced. By carrying pollen from one flower to another, the bees and butterflies helped the flowers produce seeds for new plants.

Though the butterflies were helpful, the gardener knew that their young—the caterpillars—were not. They often damaged plants by eating the leaves.

The ants and wasps in the garden were harmful in one way but helpful in another. They sometimes nibbled on ripe fruit before the gardener got around to picking it. But they also helped the garden by eating harmful insects.

There was no question about the aphids, though. The gardener knew they were bad for the garden, because they sucked plant juices and spread diseases.

He didn't know much about the bright red ladybugs, but he thought they were special and was very fond of them.

One day the gardener had an idea. If I get rid of the bad insects, he thought, my garden will be perfect. So the next day, the gardener sprayed the fruit trees, the vegetables, and the flowers. He used a spray gun filled with bug killer.

As the gardener sprayed the poison, the bees, ants, and wasps hid in their nests to protect themselves. But the ladybugs didn't have any nests, so they flew away in a great red cloud.

The aphids didn't have nests either, but, without wings, they couldn't fly away. They hid under the leaves in the garden.

When the gardener finished spraying, the aphids crept out of their hiding places and went back to work. Many of them died from the poison, but others survived.

The aphids sucked the juice out of leaves and tender plant stems. Some of the juice passed through their bodies and turned into a sweet, sticky liquid called honeydew.

Soon it seemed there were more aphids than ever before. As they multiplied, they sucked more and more plant juice. It wasn't long before the plants in the garden were coated with sticky honeydew, which ants love.

The ants "milked" the aphids by stroking them with their feelers. This made the aphids squeeze out honeydew, which the ants then licked up.

There were so many ants going to get honeydew from the aphids that the gardener began to see ant trails all over the garden.

The bees in the garden liked honeydew, too. It was easier for the bees to lick honeydew from the plants to make their honey than it was for them to go from flower to flower collecting nectar. Besides, there were fewer flowers now. The plants had become too sick to make many flowers, because of the damage the aphids had done.

With fewer flowers, there were fewer butterflies visiting the garden. But there were still many caterpillars. They stayed in the garden, eating leaves, until they grew big enough to turn into butterflies and fly away.

Not only were the plants too sick to make many flowers, the fruit trees were too sick to produce much fruit. Wasps buzzed angrily about, fighting over what little fruit there was.

And all the while, the aphids continued to multiply. There were so many, in fact, that they were crowded together on the plants, fighting one another for food and space. Many plants were so covered with honeydew that they grew mouldy.

The gardener knew that something was terribly wrong. The garden had few flowers, the fruit trees had little fruit, and the vegetables were shrivelled up and wilted. The plants were covered with aphids. There were ant hills and ant trails everywhere. The wasps were becoming a nuisance, and the butterflies had all but disappeared. Even the bees' honey tasted strange, because they had made it from honeydew instead of nectar.

The gardener didn't know what to do. He could see that spraying with poison had been a mistake. He understood now that all the life in his garden was linked somehow, that the plants and insects depended on one another to survive.

"What about ladybugs?" a friend suggested.

"What about them?" the gardener asked.

"Ladybugs are nature's way of controlling aphids," the friend replied. And she gave him an address from which to order a supply.

When the box of ladybugs arrived, the gardener took it out to the garden, opened it, and left it in a shady spot under a tree. One by one, the ladybugs flew or crawled out of the box. Soon they were all over the garden.

The ladybugs ate all the aphids they could find. They ate and ate and ate and ate. And after a while, the garden began to recover. The plants grew stronger and healthier.

When the following summer came, the gardener looked all around his garden. Once again there were hardy vegetables, brightly coloured flowers, and lots of sweet, ripe fruit. The butterflies were back. The ants and wasps had settled down. And the bees were making delicious honey. Everything was as it should be.

The gardener smiled. He had always known there was something special about ladybugs!

AFTER YOU READ

Organize information

Review the facts you learned from the story. Organize your information in a chart or a web.

BURNS

Written by Suzanne Diamond, B.Sc., M.Sc. (Botany)

READING TIP

Learn from photos

How much can you learn about Burns Bog by just looking at the photos?
Take notes as you look at the photos, and then read to find out more.

Take a Walk in a Bog

What do you think of when you hear the word "bog"? A wet marshy place where you sink into spongy moss with every step? A place where a variety of bog creatures hide in the shadows?

Well, take a walk in Burns Bog near Vancouver, and discover what a marvellous, mysterious place a bog can be. This bog is full of bird songs and flowers, clean water and fresh air. Even though Burns Bog is close to a large city, it's full of wildlife.

What Is a Bog?

Bogs, like swamps and marshes, are wetlands. Most wetlands are low places where water collects in ponds and streams, like the Prairie potholes in Canada's western provinces. Burns Bog is a special kind of wetland called a *raised bog*. That means that it rises above the flat land around it like a dome. At the top, the dome is as high as a two-storey building, about 5 m.

The amazing thing about a raised bog is that it still has lily ponds on top, and clumps of soggy moss called *sphagnum moss*. This moss can hold 30 times its own mass in water.

116

BOG

LEARNING GOALS

You will

- learn why bogs are important
- use photos to find information

How Burns Bog Was Formed

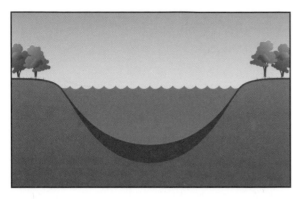

7000–15 000 Years Ago

The story of Burns Bog goes back 15 000 years. At that time, glaciers 1500 m deep covered British Columbia's Lower Mainland. As the ice melted, it left a hollow in the land that became a tidal flat.

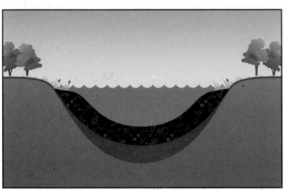

5000 Years Ago

Cattails, grasses, and other marsh plants began to grow in the tidal flat.

4000 Years Ago

Decomposing plants built up a layer of peat.

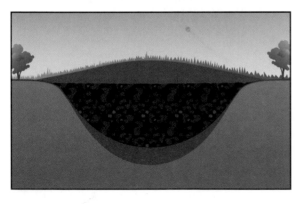

3000 Years Ago

Plants, trees, shrubs, and mosses grew on the peat. The layers of new peat formed into a raised bog approximately 5 m above sea level at the centre and 1.5 m above sea level at its edges.

How a Raised Bog Is Formed

How did Burns Bog become a raised bog? It all started during the last Ice Age, when British Columbia was a cold place covered with a thick layer of ice. This ice was called a glacier, and in places it was more than a kilometre thick!

As British Columbia got warmer, the ice melted. In the delta of the Fraser River it left a hollow place, or depression. Grass and cattails grew up in the hollow. Over thousands of years their decaying remains formed layer after layer of peat. Moss, shrubs, and trees grew on the peat and slowly raised the surface of the bog.

A Giant Sponge

Peat is wonderful stuff. We use it in the garden to make the soil rich and loose. Over a hundred years ago, people who lived near Burns Bog dug up the peat, dried it, and burned it in their homes as fuel.

These days we know that it is not wise to harvest the peat in a bog for fuel. Bogs may be squishy, but they act like huge sponges, soaking up excess water that might flood nearby areas. The plants that grow on the bog also filter the water, making it pure and sweet. The oxygen plants give off helps us breathe. Let's look at some of the plants in Burns Bog.

This is a satellite photo of Burns Bog.

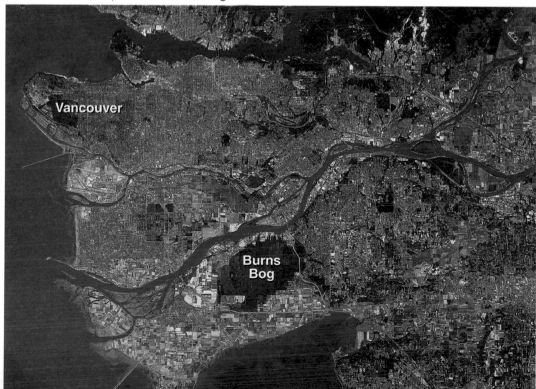

The Plants of Burns Bog

Aboriginal peoples have used the plants of Burns Bog for food and medicine for more than 5000 years. There are delicious wild cranberries, blueberries, and cloudberries. There are water lilies blooming in the ponds and Labrador Tea with its sweet-smelling flowers. There are small pine trees and even carnivorous plants that eat insects.

The plants in Burns Bog are part of a very special ecosystem. Bogs produce more oxygen than forests do. That means local bogs supply extra fresh air for the surrounding environments. Bogs can also store carbon dioxide—more than 20 times as much as a rain forest! This is important because carbon dioxide and other greenhouse gases cause global warming. For people in cities, this fresh air is important.

Animal Life

If you walked along the boardwalk at Burns Bog, you would see insects buzz and hum around the flowers. You might see a frog hop into a lily pond or a salamander sunning itself. All these species of insects and animals provide food for larger birds and animals.

The water and plants of the bog provide a lush home for many species of animals. Some, like beavers, are common. Others, like greater sandhill cranes, are so rare they are threatened with extinction. At least two pairs of greater sandhill cranes have nested in Burns Bog. These large cranes are so special that the

beavers. Overhead soar eagles, falcons, merlins, kestrels, and trumpeter swans.

The Pacific Flyway

Aboriginal peoples of British Columbia think of them as good luck signs.

In and around the bog run important salmon streams. The bog helps keep the water at the right temperature for the fish.

On a walk through the bog you might see bears, red foxes, black-tailed deer, and

Some of the birds in Burns Bog are visitors. They stop here on their way south for the winter or north for the summer. The Burns Bog area is part of the route used by migrating birds—the Pacific Flyway. Ducks and other waterfowl live in lagoons that look like small lakes. These lagoons were left by the people who dug peat from Burns Bog long ago.

Protecting Burns Bog

Luckily, the lumpy, watery surface of the bog has made it hard to make roads through Burns Bog, or build houses or shopping plazas. Recently, however, people have suggested clearing the bog to make a golf course, using it as a dump, or running a six-lane highway through the middle.

Other people want to protect the bog as a wilderness park. Peatlands are very rare in the world and only one in a million is a raised bog like

Burns Bog. People who want to save the bog point to all the good things this special ecosystem does to preserve plant life, animal life—and even human life.

Part of Burns Bog is now protected and called the Delta Nature Reserve. Volunteers of the Burns Bog Conservation Society give visitors guided tours. When unique environments like Burns Bog are protected, visitors can explore and observe why these areas are so special to our world.

Key Wetland Areas in Canada

YUKON TERRITORY

NORTHWEST TERRITORIES

NUNAVUT

BRITISH COLUMBIA

ALBERTA

MANITOBA

NEWFOUNDLAND

Burns Bog

SASKATCHEWAN

ONTARIO

QUEBEC

PRINCE EDWARD ISLAND

NEW BRUNSWICK

NOVA SCOTIA

AFTER YOU READ

Think about your learning

Review the notes you took as you looked at the photos. How did the photos help you understand the information?

EXPLORE AND OBSERVE

In this unit, you have learned how others observe the world around them. Look around at *your* world. Become an observer and create your own observation report or project.

BEFORE YOU BEGIN

Choose something to observe from the world of nature. Be sure that it is easy and safe to observe every day at the same time for five days. What you have chosen to observe is called the *subject*.

- Does it do anything unusual or unexpected?
- What are its habits?
- How does it eat?
- What does it look like?

Decide how to record your observations. You could use a diary or a log. You might want to draw pictures, or take photos or videos.

Pick Me!
- a pet
- an anthill
- a bird
- your choice!

Kaitlin decided to use a log like this one for each day.

Subject: My Hamster			
Day: 1		Day: 2	
Date:		Date:	
Time:	Observations:	Time:	Observations:
7 p.m.		7 p.m.	
8 p.m.		8 p.m.	

124

MAKING YOUR OBSERVATIONS

- Observe your subject and record your observations in your observation log. Make sure you watch your subject at the same time every day.
- Try to tell exactly what you see, hear, and smell. Use specific words so you will be able to remember details later.

Here are Kaitlin's observation notes.

Subject: My Hamster								
Day: 1			Day: 2			Day: 3		
Date: Oct. 12			Date: Oct. 13			Date: Oct. 14		
Time:	Observations:		Time:	Observations:		Time:	Observations:	
7 p.m.	wakes up, moves shavings, stretches, goes to water		7 p.m.	wakes up, moves shavings, stretches, goes to water		7 p.m.	wakes up, moves shavings, stretches, goes to water	
8 p.m.	rides on wheel, eats		8 p.m.	eats, runs up tubes		8 p.m.	rides on wheel	

Remember to draw pictures or take photos or videotapes as you observe.

My Findings

- wakes up early in the evening
- licks paws, pushes bedding around
- eats and drinks
- runs on exercise wheel
- up at night
- sleeps during the day

What Did You Discover?

- Read through your notes. Look at your diagrams and photos.
- Did you notice any patterns?
- How were your questions answered?
- Make a list of your findings.

YOUR FIRST DRAFT

1. Start Your Report

- Record some information about your subject. What is it? Where did you observe it? What time did you make your observation?

- Tell what you observed. What patterns did you notice? What was unusual about your subject?

Observing My Hamster

by Kaitlin Franek

I observed my hamster Bob every day for a week. Each day was the same. The hamster is in my bedroom and he has a big cage with tubes to go to other parts of the cage.

It is early evening. The hamster in my bedroom is beginning to wake up. He licks his paws and pushes the bedding around. After a short walk to the water bottle, he goes to look for food. This hamster seems happy to be up. Thirsty, he goes to the water bottle, and then hungry, looks for his food dish. He then goes to his wheel and exercises by running. He must like to run a lot because he runs all the time. My hamster is up at night and sleeps in the day. He is a nocturnal animal.

You might want to include a section that tells why you think your subject acted this way. The hamster did not tell Kaitlin he was hungry or thirsty. Kaitlin inferred that from her own observations, and put her findings in her report.

2. Put It All Together

Decide what would be the best way to tell your reader what you observed.

Kaitlin put her report in a file folder. She included her charts, diagrams, and logs, and made labels for each.

Observation Report

Kaitlin

REVISE AND EDIT

Go back and review your observation report.

- Ask a classmate or friend to look at your work. Listen to their suggestions. Are there ways to improve what you've done?

- Proofread your work for errors in spelling, punctuation, and grammar.

- Have you used complete sentences? capital letters for names and sentence beginnings? periods or question marks at the end of sentences or questions?

Ways to Share Your Observations

- a booklet
- a poster
- an electronic file
- a video
- photos
- diagrams

Think About Your Learning

Add other ideas to these to help you write a good observation report.

- Is the subject easy to observe?
- Does my report have a beginning, a middle, and an end?
- Do I give enough detail to make the reader feel like they were observing with me?
- Are there diagrams, photos, videos, or tapes of my research?

Unit 3: *Media Close-up*

Have you ever noticed how the media is all around you: radio, television, advertising, videos, movies, and newspapers? In this unit, you will find out how some of this media is created. You will also learn how to look more closely at media products so that you will become a better viewer. You will

- read pictures and images for information and enjoyment
- find out how some media products are created
- understand how camera angles can change the way you see a picture
- think about how characters on television are not always like people in real life
- become aware that there are many different kinds of advertising
- create media products of your own

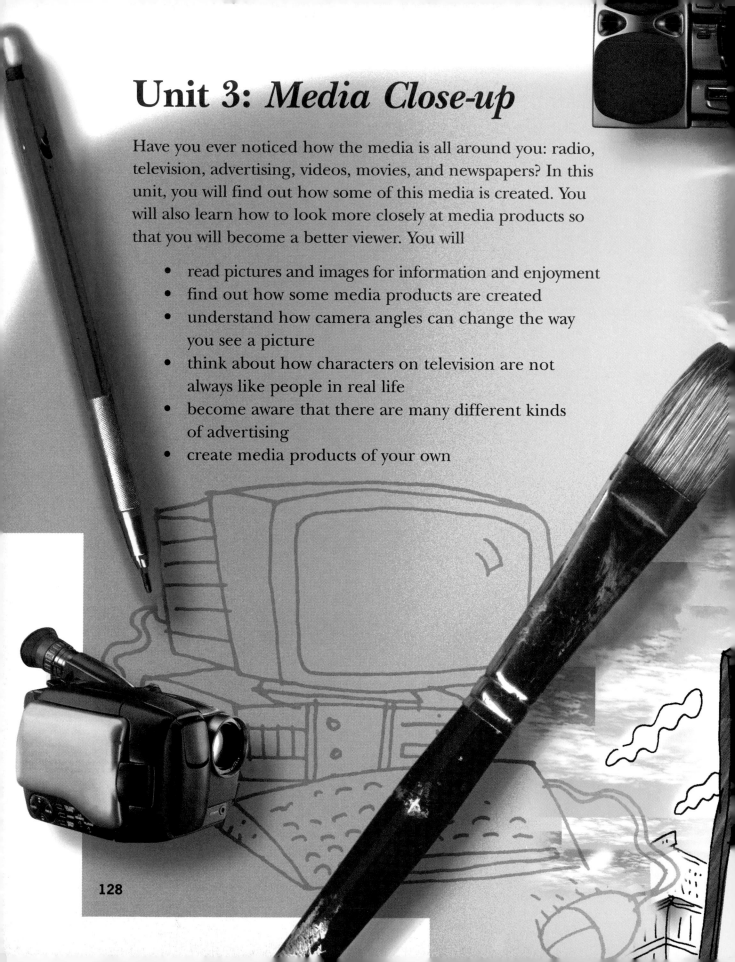

RED RAVEN

Written by Todd Mercer

COMIC BOOK
SUPERHERO

READING TIP

Think about what you know

Thinking about what you already know about a topic can
help you to read a selection. Make a chart and record in
the "Before Reading" column what you already know about
superheroes and making comic books.

Before Reading	After Reading

Red Raven was created by Charles Fiddler of The
Pas, Manitoba. As a child, Charles Fiddler liked drawing and
reading comic books. He always dreamed of becoming a
comic book artist and writer when he grew up.

When in his twenties, Charles became a commercial
artist. A few years later, he thought, "I can learn to combine
my drawing and writing skills to create comic books."

LEARNING GOALS

You will

- learn how a comic book is created
- compare new information to what you already know

Charles used his First Nations background to create his first comic book, *Red Raven: Lore of the Time Before.* Like Wonder Woman and Superman, Red Raven is a superhero. A stone with special powers lets him change from the Cree warrior, Lynx, into Red Raven, "enemy of evil."

I talked with Charles Fiddler about creating comic books.

Charles, where do your character and story ideas come from?

Many of my comic book characters and ideas come from Native stories. For example, as a child, I remember being told stories about a creature called the Wendigo. He could change shapes so he was called a shape shifter. In my comic, *Lore of the Time Before,* there's a character named Wetigou who is a scary creature like the Wendigo.

To retell Native stories, I invented a main character who could travel around North America. Red Raven has adventures with Native peoples from the past.

Do you research First Nations cultures before creating your stories?

Yes, I use a lot of reference books to get descriptions of major characters. Often I read traditional stories to check that the information in these books is correct.

Did research help you draw the comic book pictures?

Research helped when I was drawing the Native village. But when I was drawing characters from Native myths, I had to fill in the details myself.

Why do you include a map in your Red Raven comic book?

In superhero comic books, it's very important to give the story a background. For example, in the Conan comic books there's a map of where the make-believe superhero lives. Red Raven's home is an Opaskwayak Cree village. This village really did exist.

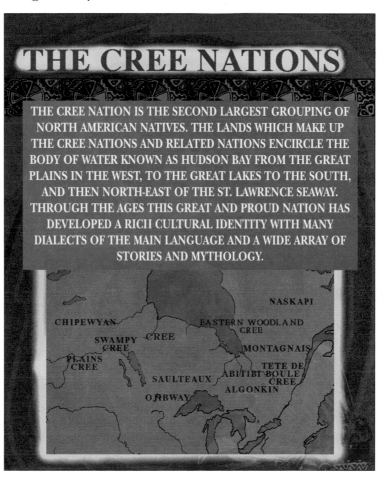

The Cree Nation is the second largest Aboriginal nation in North America.

How is a comic book created?

1. Charles starts by drawing rough sketches. He then creates black-and-white drawings.

2. Charles adds colour to the drawings.

3. After Charles adds the captions, the completed comic book is printed. Shown here is a press sheet containing eight pages of the printed comic book.

Is your band, the Opaskwayak Cree Nation, involved in your work?

The band is a partner in my company, Bold Ink Graphics. They trust me to represent Native culture in my comic books. But when I need help or advice, they're always there.

Why do you think it's important to have Native characters and stories featured in comic books?

For many years, people passed these stories on from grandparents to grandchildren. But today, the family is sometimes not as strong. So the stories are being lost. One of the best things I can do is keep these important Native stories alive by presenting them in my comic books.

AFTER YOU READ

Compare new information

List what you learned while reading this selection in the "After Reading" column of your chart. Compare your two lists. What new information did you learn?

135

Make a FLIPBOOK

Written by Patrick Jenkins
Illustrated by Dave Whamond

READING TIP

Scan headings

Text that tells you how to do something is organized so that the reader knows what to do first, second, third, and so on. Look at the headings in this selection to find out how to make a flip book.

How Flipbooks Work

An animated cartoon is a series of pictures one after the other. Look closely at the strip of movie film shown on the following page. Each drawing of the bird is a bit different from the one before. When these pictures, or frames, are flashed quickly in front of your eyes, the bird appears to fly. In a cartoon movie, you see 24 pictures every second! That means that during a 90-minute movie like *Aladdin,* you watch about 130 000 pictures.

You can make your own movie in a flipbook—but don't worry, you won't have to draw 130 000 pictures. A flipbook is a small pad of paper with a drawing on each page. Just like the frames of a filmstrip, each drawing in a flipbook is a little bit different from the one before. When you flip the pages, it's almost like watching a short animated movie.

Follow the five steps that follow, and then you'll be ready to make your own flipbook.

· ·

1. Get a pad

Use a small notepad to make your flipbook. Pads that are about 8 cm x 13 cm work well. Your pad should have at least 50 pages—96 pages is ideal. Plain white paper works best.

Always work from the back of the pad to the front. When you are ready to flip the pad, you will flip from the back to the front.

LEARNING GOALS

You will

- find out how animation is created
- read to follow directions

Keep your drawings near the open edge of the pad.

It is best to keep your pictures on the half of the page closest to the open edge. This will make them easy to see when you flip the pages of your flipbook.

2. Draw a character

Keep your character simple! Use simple shapes, such as circles, squares, and triangles. Look at the drawings below. These simple characters will be easy to draw over and over again.

3. Use a stencil

A stencil is a drawing of your character that you can trace. The stencil helps you keep your character the same size and shape in each drawing.

Go over the lines on your stencil drawing with a black pen or marker. Place each page of the flipbook on top of your stencil to trace it. You will need to be able to see your stencil through the page. Hold the stencil in place as you draw so that it doesn't move.

4. Move your character

The secret to smooth animation is to move your character just a tiny bit between pages. Move your stencil about the width of a toothpick (2 mm) each time.

Do your flipbook animation in pencil first. That way you can fix any mistakes.

Go over the outlines of your characters with a fine black marker. This will make your animation easy to see.

Move your stencil about the width of a toothpick (2 mm).

5. Flip the pages to watch your movie!

Check your movie every now and then to make sure the animation is working. Just flip your pages. Usually you'll need to do at least 10 drawings before you can see movement. Your movie will become more and more interesting as you add more pages.

Have fun!

AFTER YOU READ

Make a flow chart

When you read to follow directions, it is important to follow each step carefully and in the right order. Make a flow chart to help you remember the directions.

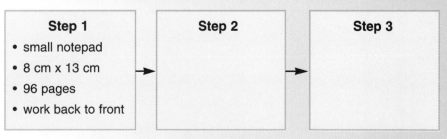

Step 1	Step 2	Step 3
• small notepad • 8 cm x 13 cm • 96 pages • work back to front		

FANTASY

Written by Miranda Alexander
Illustrated by Kathryn Adams

READING TIP

Find the main ideas

In many information selections, headings tell you the main ideas. As you read this selection, find the main idea for each section.

Have you ever wondered how your favourite TV and movie cartoons are made? This short "walking tour" of an animation studio introduces you to some of the many artists who work together to create a cartoon.

Writers

Animation begins with the writers. They think of funny situations for the cartoon characters. They get together to brainstorm ideas for a story. Often they post their ideas on a wall using index cards or coloured paper. That way they can reorganize the events in their story. After they develop the basic story idea, they write a working script.

STUDIOS

Storyboard Artists

Storyboard artists take the working script and sketch it out in a storyboard. A storyboard is a series of rough drawings that shows the main events in the story.

Layout Artists

Layout artists make more detailed drawings of the characters. They show how characters look and move. They also focus on the expressions on the characters' faces.

LEARNING GOALS

You will

- learn how cartoons are made
- find main ideas

Background Artists

A background is a stage for the characters to act in. This background artist is working on a background scene that can be used over and over again.

Animators

Once the character drawings and script are done, the animators begin their work. Some animators draw each frame of the cartoon. There are 24 frames for every *second* in a movie cartoon! At first, the animation is done in pencil. The animators can "test" the characters' movements by flipping pages. Then, they trace and paint the drawings on plastic sheets called *cels*. Today, much of the animators' work can be done by computer.

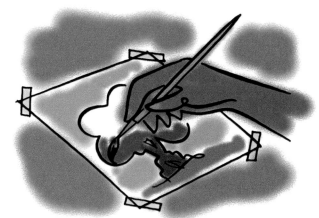

When creating movement, computer animators use the drawing tool of their computer program to set up the first and last positions in the animation sequence. These are the first and last robot figures in the illustration below.

To make the robot's knee move, computer animators set up the first position and the end position of the movement. The computer figures out and draws the positions in between. The shaded parts in the picture below are called *in-betweens*. Before computers, all animators had to draw each cel by hand.

These figures were all created using computer animation.

Voice Artists

While the layout artists work on how the characters look, the voice artists work on how the characters sound. They record the dialogue in the script.

Musicians and Special Effects Artists

Finally, cartoons need music and sound effects to give the story energy. (Just try watching a cartoon *without* the sound on.) Musicians compose and record music to match the action in the cartoon. They add those little musical "jabs"—BLINKS, BOINGS, and CRASHES. Other artists provide the cool sound effects, such as footsteps, crashes, thunder, and rain.

Ta-Da! Mix all of these things together, and you've got a cartoon!

AFTER YOU READ

Make a summary

A summary of main ideas can help you to remember the information of a selection. Make a list of the headings in this selection. Beside each heading, write a phrase or sentence that tells you what the section is about.

Get the Picture!

Written by Alan Simpson
Illustrated by Tina Holdcroft

READING TIP

Compare photographs to get information

Look carefully at the photographs in the section titled "Distance." What is different about each photo? What is the same? What do you think the text beside the photos will be about? Look at the photographs for the next two sections and ask yourself the same questions.

Taking photographs is a great way to capture special or interesting moments. First you must decide *what* type of picture you will shoot. Will it be a person? a pet? a building? Then you need to think about *how* to set up for the shot.

Good photographers compose their pictures with the audience and purpose in mind.

In this article, you will read about some things you can do to create a variety of photographic effects.

LEARNING GOALS

You will

- find out how using a camera in different ways can change photographs
- compare photographs taken from different angles and distances

Distance

The distance of your camera from the subject of the shot changes the way your audience will react to your photographs.

You can move in on a subject to take a *close-up*. A close-up shot lets your audience share the feelings of the subject.

You can stand back from your subject to take a *long shot*. A long shot lets you show more details.

You can also take a *medium shot*. A medium shot will let your audience see all of the main subject and a few of the details in the background.

Camera Angles

When you place your camera at *eye level* with a subject, your audience will see its normal shape and proportion.

If you take a *low-angle shot,* your subject will seem "larger than life." For a low-angle shot, you place your camera below the subject so that the audience will be looking up at it.

A *high-angle shot* is taken from above the subject. When you use this shot, the subject will look smaller than its surroundings.

Composition

Sometimes you can arrange, or *compose*, the different elements in a picture. Placing an element in front—in the *foreground*—may give it special emphasis.

Placing the same element in the background will create a different effect.

Now that you know some photography basics you can experiment. See how changing camera distances, camera angles, and photo composition can affect your pictures. Have fun!

AFTER YOU READ

Use what you have learned

Collect photographs from magazines and newspapers. Explain how the camera was used to create the pictures.

MADE-IN-CANADA

Computer Effects

Written by Elizabeth St. Philip

Canadian computer animator Bob Gundu is finishing work on a 30-second car commercial. The car will leap off a bridge, fly through the air, and land on a ferry. With computer imaging, anything is possible.

Gundu starts with a video of the real car attached to cables and lifted into the air by cranes.

"My job is to erase all the wire cables from the shot," says Gundu. Other animators add bubbles to the water and paint fluffier clouds.

The ability to use both reality and computer effects has changed the way that movies, TV shows, and commercials are made. When an image is computerized, it becomes a series of tiny dots called *pixels*. Computer artists can do whatever they want with these pixels. It is now hard to tell real images from the images changed by computer.

LEARNING GOALS

You will

- find out how special effects are created
- preview the selection to get an overall picture of what the selection is about

Computer animator Bob Gundu.

Thousands of dots called *pixels* make up one image.

⬆ This beach scene shown above was changed to the one below using computer technology. ⬇

154

In the movie *Jumanji,* a live herd of elephants appears to be running with a crowd of people. This special effect is an exciting example of Canadian creativity at work. The 3-D image of the elephant was created by a company called Alias/Wavefront in Toronto. The computer animation program that made the image move came from Softimage in Montreal. Alias/Wavefront also produced software to create special effects for the movies *Batman Forever* and *Jurassic Park.*

Canada is well known for its computer artists and computer animation training programs. Many entertainment companies from around the world come to Ontario's Sheridan College to hire its graduates. Sheridan's most famous graduate, Steve Williams, created the dinosaurs in *Jurassic Park* and some of the dazzling effects in *The Mask.*

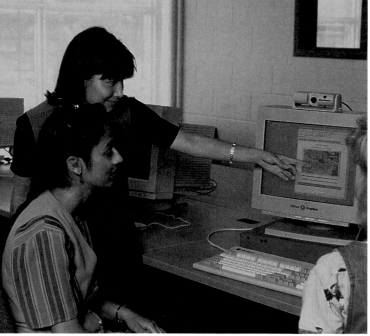

If you are interested in becoming a computer artist, Canada is one of the best places to be. We can all be proud of the Canadian talent who are leading the way in developing computer special effects.

Computer animation students at Sheridan College.

CREATING

Your Own

SPECIAL EFFECTS

If you have access to a video camera, either at home or at school, try this:

Cut a star shape out of a piece of cardboard. Fix the piece of cardboard with the star-shaped hole over the lens. Whatever you film will then be seen inside the star. Or smear an ordinary glass filter with grease to create a misty effect.

If your camera has a pause button, try this:

Film someone holding a book. Press pause and remove the book, telling the person not to move a muscle. Begin filming again. When you view your film, it will look as if the book disappeared.

(Hint: It helps if the person looks confused after the book is taken away.)

AFTER YOU READ

Think about your learning

Look back at your predictions. How well did your predictions match what the selection was about? Did skimming help you to make good predictions?

Song of the Open Road

Written by Ogden Nash
Illustrated by Kim LaFave

I think that I shall never see
A billboard lovely as a tree.
Indeed, unless the billboards fall
I'll never see a tree at all.

TUBE TIME

Written by Eve Merriam   Illustrated by Sean Dawdy

I turned on the TV
and what did I see?

I saw a can of cat food talking,
a tube of toothpaste walking.

Peanuts, popcorn,
cotton flannel.
Jump up, jump up,
switch the channel.

I turned to station B
and what did I see?

I saw a shampoo bottle crying,
a pile of laundry flying.

Peanuts, popcorn,
cotton flannel.
Jump up, jump up,
switch the channel.

I turned to station D
and what did I see?

I saw two spray cans warring,
a cup of coffee snoring.

    Peanuts, popcorn,
    cotton flannel.
    Jump up, jump up,
    switch the channel.

I turned to station E
and what did I see?

I saw dancing fingers dialing,
an upset stomach smiling.

    Peanuts, popcorn,
    cotton flannelette:
    Jump up, jump up,
    turn off the set.

Welcome to TV LAND!

Written by Shelagh Wallace
Illustrated by Ken Phipps

READING TIP

Use clues to figure out new words

Authors often try to explain difficult words by giving clues, such as a definition or a picture. As you read, note what clues this author gives to help you figure out new words.

You're about to enter TV Land—that familiar, yet oh-so-unusual place where TV characters live. You've got the couch to yourself, the cushions just right, and sole control of the remote. As you surf through dozens of channels, you are able to identify, in just seconds, the different kinds of programs that are on. Wait a minute—how do you do all of that so fast?

Tune in to the Details

You, along with millions of other TV viewers, understand what you see on TV because it uses *conventions:* widely recognized details and ways of doing things that you accept and understand as being part of particular TV shows. Conventions help you quickly tell what's going on, and that's important. After you take out the commercials, half-hour programs have only 22 minutes to tell a story, and hour-long programs have just 48 minutes.

Of course, when you're watching TV, the conventions are so familiar that you don't

What kinds of shows are shown here? How do you know?

LEARNING GOALS

You will

- read about how some TV shows are created
- find out why some TV characters are not like people in real life
- use clues to figure out new words

notice them. But what happens if you listen to the TV with your eyes closed? Just by listening, you'll recognize some shows by some of their particular details and ways of doing things. You'll pick out a comedy by the audience's laughter, a drama by its suspenseful music and the actors' solemn tones, and a game show by the announcer's voice and the constant bells and buzzers.

Meet Some Very Familiar Faces

Like conventions, standard character types, or *stereotypes,* are used on TV because viewers quickly and easily recognize them. For instance, as soon as you see an awkward character with weird clothes and glasses, you instantly think that this character is smart but nerdy. The show's writers don't need to spend a lot of time explaining that he or she is rather clever at school but uncomfortable with people.

You've probably seen other TV stereotypes, such as the goofy best friend who causes problems; the all-knowing, always understanding parents; or the bothersome little sister or brother. Stereotyped TV characters are often exaggerations of certain kinds of people. On the other hand, most stereotypes aren't at all like people in real life. Is there a stereotype on TV that is similar to you and just as interesting and complex as you are?

AFTER YOU READ

Make a list

Make a list of your new words. Beside each word, write the clue you found that helped you figure out what the word means.

LIGHTS! CAMERA! ACTION!

Written by Susan Green
Illustrated by Richard Hockney

READING TIP

Ask questions

Make a list of what you already know about how cameras are used to make TV programs. What else would you like to know? Write down two or three questions. As you read, look for the answers.

Do you ever wonder about what goes on behind the scenes when a TV program is made? Here is a look at what you see on your TV screen and the people and technology that make it happen.

LEARNING GOALS

You will

- read and view pictures about filming TV programs

- ask questions and give proof for your answers

Most of what we see on TV drama shows looks real.

166

The scene for the story is usually set with a wide shot.

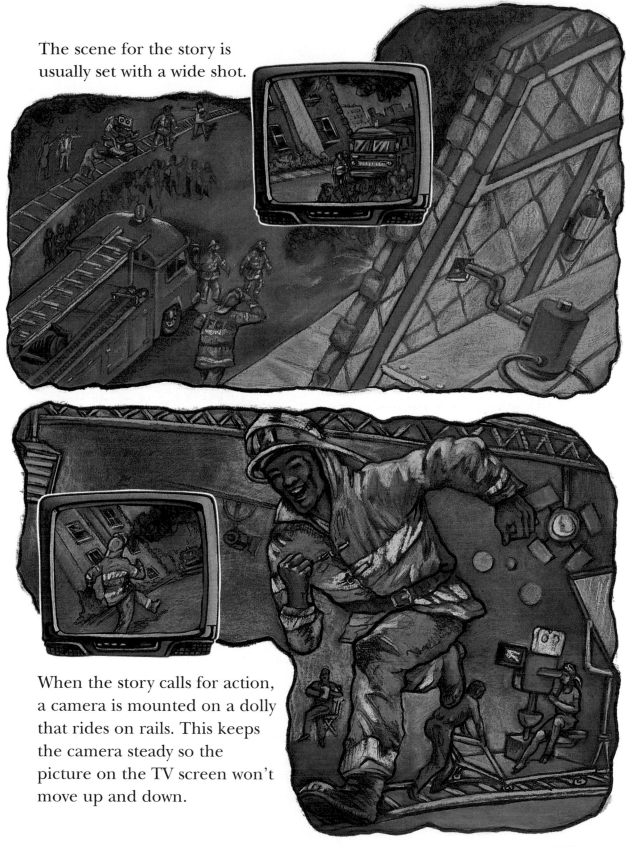

When the story calls for action, a camera is mounted on a dolly that rides on rails. This keeps the camera steady so the picture on the TV screen won't move up and down.

When something exciting or scary happens to the actor in the story, you often see a reaction shot or close-up.

When shots don't feature an actor's face, a stand-in actor is used.

In dangerous or physically challenging scenes, stunt people often replace the actors. They dress up to look like the actors in the camera shots.

When all of the camera work is done, the different camera shots are put together to make the program you see on your TV screen.

AFTER YOU READ

Find proof

Record the answers to your questions. How did you find the answers? Did you change your mind about anything you wrote on your "What I Already Know" list?

Hiccup Champion

OF THE WORLD

Written by Ken Roberts

Excerpted from the novel Hiccup Champion of the World

Illustrated by Tadeusz Majewski

Maynard Chan has had the hiccups for three months.

Now he is becoming well known for his problem.

When I got home from school, Mom was standing in
the living room waiting for me. She was excited.

"Guess who called today, honey?" she said.

Mom never makes me guess bad news. She just blurts
it out. And she never calls me "honey" unless I've done
something right.

LEARNING GOALS

You will

- read about a boy who is a guest on a TV talk show

- compare your experiences with those of a story character

"You've got good news about ... hic ... me," I said.

Mom looked stunned.

"That's right. How did you know?"

I shrugged, trying to think of what I'd been doing to cause a good phone call. All I'd been doing was hiccuping.

"Henry Rendall called." Mom said the name slowly, like this person Henry Rendall was somebody important.

"Who?"

"Henry Rendall," Mom repeated, still with a silly grin.

"Who is Henry Rendall?"

"You don't know the King of Late Night Television Talk Shows?" Her hands were spread out, faced upward like she was checking for rain.

"What time does he ... hic ... come on, Mom?"

"Midnight."

"And what's my bedtime?"

"Nine p.m."

"So how am I supposed to know about the King of Late Night Television?"

"Don't you read? He's in all the gossip magazines."

"You don't let me ... hic ... read gossip magazines."

Mom got mad.

When Mom's mad, she doesn't say a word for exactly five minutes. It's something she learned in some workshop. She sits down and stares at the clock on our living-room wall. The clock is a giant plastic pig. The hands circle the pig's oversized snout, the month appears in one nostril and the date in the other. The curly tail ticks out seconds.

I memorized the exact time Mom started staring, went to the kitchen, poured myself a glass of milk, and then came back to the living room to sip milk until the five minutes were up.

"What did this Henry Rendall guy say?" I asked as the second hand raced past the left nostril.

"He didn't say anything," Mom said. She was still mad and had obviously decided to make me work for answers.

"Then how'd you know ... hic ... it was him?"

"I didn't talk with Henry Rendall himself, silly. He has better things to do. I talked with one of his writers, Mr. Richardson."

"What does this Mr. Richardson want?" I asked, finishing my milk.

"He wants you, silly," said Mom, getting excited again.

"Me?"

"He read about you in the paper and wants you to be on the Henry Rendall Show, coast to coast. Millions of people will see you. Hiccup Champion of the World!"

I wasn't thrilled like Mom wanted me to be. I was mad. This television show wanted me because my hiccups were funny. I was tired of people laughing at hiccups. They'd probably try to scare me, right on television. They'd make me put my head in a paper bag and stand upside down and everything.

"I won't do it, Mom."

She didn't panic.

"Why not, Maynard?"

"I'm not Hiccup Champion of the World. Some guy ... hic ... hiccuped for more than sixty years."

"Where is he now?"

"He died."

"So, you're the champ."

"There's a girl in Florida ... hic ... who hiccuped for two years. She's still alive."

"Hiccuping?"

"No. But there must be somebody in India or South America or ...."

"Maynard, listen to me. It doesn't matter if you're really Hiccup Champion of the World. That's just television. Think about this, though. Has anyone you know ever been on national television?"

"Denise Bonin."

"Doing what?"

"She was standing in the crowd during a parade."

"And she still talks about it, right?"

"Yeah."

"You won't be somebody in a crowd, Maynard. You'll be a star."

"And they'll be laughing at ... hic ... me, Mom."

"Is that what you're afraid of, Maynard?"

Mom uses my name a lot when she's trying to talk me
into something. I shrugged and nodded. She came and sat
beside me, hugging me gently like she did when I was little.

"Nobody will laugh at you, Maynard."

"Yes, they will."

"No. You can go on national television and show
people that you're brave ...."

"I'm not brave."

"... and witty ..."

"I'm not ... hic ... witty."

"People love to watch someone with troubles who is still happy and bright and charming. You're all those things, Maynard."

Mom leaned over and kissed me on the forehead.

"But I'm not ...."

"Pretend," said Mom, exasperated. "This is big-time television. Television is a pretend world. Pretend for ten short minutes, and you'll be a rich little star."

"Rich?"

Mom's eyes twinkled.

"Oh, silly me. Didn't I mention that the Henry Rendall Show will pay for both of us to fly to Toronto? They'll pay for all our meals and our hotel bills, and they'll give you $1000 appearance money."

I tried to imagine what it would be like on national television. I could hear myself being introduced and see the curtain part. I could hear the roar of the studio audience as I grinned calmly and waved. I could see movie stars standing next to Henry Rendall. It was a little too fuzzy to tell which stars, but they were famous and they were clapping frantically as I sat down. I could hear myself hiccup and then smile as everyone cheered again. Hiccup Champion of the World.

I'd rather be rodeo champion or skateboard champion or spelling champion, but at least I was champion of something. It had been a hard three months. I had earned my chance for glory and fame.

"Mom?" I said.

"Yeah?"

"I'll do it."

What a mistake.

The studio was a big disappointment. It wasn't fancy at all. I'd pictured some mansion surrounded by grass and a high iron fence to keep out hordes of fans. Instead it's a converted warehouse next to an underpants factory. The only person on the street was a woman waiting for a bus. The guard at the front door sent Mom to the audience and me to a guest dressing room. A woman, Monique, put powder on me so the lights wouldn't make my skin shine. Mr. Richardson, a nice guy but busy, came in and told me a dozen times not to be nervous. He made me nervous.

"I'm scared," I said.

"Of course," said Mr. Richardson, smiling at me and patting me on the shoulder. "That's normal. Don't worry. You'll be great. I have to go now and type up some questions for Henry to ask you. I'll come and get you in about twenty-five minutes."

He left me alone.

There are different kinds of fears. Horror movies and seances scare me. I shiver and scream. I sweat and quake.

There is another kind of fear, though. The fear of making a fool of yourself in front of people. I had never been truly afraid until Mr. Richardson said, "Don't worry" and closed the dressing-room door with a snap, leaving me alone, staring at a mirror with makeup on my face. I guess for me there is no fear like the fear of knowing I will be seen by millions and millions of people, watched and inspected. There is no fear like the fear of knowing this event will be recorded on home VCRs by every relative I have so that it can be played and replayed, again and again, not only for everyone I know but for everyone I haven't even met yet, for any children I might have, years from being born.

As soon as Mr. Richardson closed the door and left me alone, I stopped hiccuping.

I didn't even notice at first. I turned to the makeup mirror and practised answering questions. When I was tired of answering my own questions, I practised walking over to a stuffed chair and sitting down. I practised sitting various ways, so I'd look comfortable but not lazy, attentive but not stiff. Then I decided to practise how I'd smile after the audience laughed at my hiccuping. I waited for a hiccup. After about a minute I could feel sweat beginning to form along my spine. I wasn't hiccuping.

For months all I've been dreaming about is the moment my hiccups would stop, but here, in this dressing room, I want hiccups back, fast.

Five minutes from now Mr. Richardson is going to
come through that dressing-room door and scoot me out to
face a live audience so my hiccups can be taped for national
television. But I'm just another ordinary kid sitting here
listening to the air conditioner hum. My mind spinning in
circles, trying to figure out what to do.

The Henry Rendall Show has paid all our expenses.
Will I have to pay the money back if I can't hiccup? What
will Grandpa and Aunt Louise and every kid at school say
if I'm not on national television? What happens if I go out
there and admit my hiccups are gone, that after thousands

of attempts to scare them away it took Henry Rendall
to make my hiccups vanish?

Mom says television is just pretend, so maybe, since
TV wants the Hiccup Champion of the World, I should just
fake the hiccups. What difference would a few more minutes
make? Henry Rendall would have his interview, and I
wouldn't have to pay back any money. Can I remember to
hiccup on purpose for the whole interview? What if I forget?
What if I do pretend and get away with it? I can't stop after
the show. If I do, then people would know I was faking the
hiccups on TV. How long would I have to keep faking
hiccups?

Do I lie or tell the truth?

The door swings open.

"Let's go, champ," says Mr. Richardson.

"Ready," I say with a forced smile. "Let's go."

Mr. Richardson holds the door open for me, and I walk past him down the long corridor leading to the studio.

"Who's he?" one of the stage hands asks, pointing at me as we stop behind a curtain. I can hear the studio audience clapping on the other side.

"Hiccup Champion of the World," whispers Mr. Richardson.

"Hic!" I say.

Everyone makes mistakes.

One of the problems with growing up is that sometimes my mistakes are whoppers. They can't be shrugged off with a smile. But of all my whoppers, there hasn't been one that backfired as badly as the one I made when I faked my first hiccup.

"Our next guest," said Henry Rendall from the other side of the curtain, "is from Vancouver, British Columbia. He is the Hiccup Champion of the World. Let's welcome twelve-year-old Maynard Chan."

Mr. Richardson pulled back the curtain, and I walked into the bright lights. I could barely see, but I could hear the audience cheer. I stood in front of the curtain and hiccuped on purpose. People laughed. I hiccuped again and put one hand over my mouth, like people do after making some rude noise by accident. The audience cheered.

I looked over to the right. Henry Rendall stood up, waving me over to him. Next to him stood Biff Newsome, my favourite singer. I couldn't believe it. Biff Newsome, clapping for me. I walked right past Henry Rendall and shook hands with Biff Newsome. He's shorter than I thought, and older. I remembered to hiccup and then pulled out a pencil and paper so Biff could give me his autograph. I call him Biff now. He said I could while turning me around so he could use my back as a desk. The audience cheered again. I sat down, sandwiched between Henry Rendall and Biff. Henry Rendall kept trying to ask me something, but every time, mid-question, my head would swivel around toward Biff. I kept grinning like I'd just been handed a report card with straight As.

"It looks to me like you've got a fan there, Biff," said Henry Rendall.

Biff smiled and looked straight at me. "Listen here, Maynard," he said, "I've had my time in the spotlight. It's your turn now. Go on, do your bit."

My bit was hiccuping, so I did, smiling to myself. Mom had set our video machine to tape the show, in case we didn't get home in time. I could watch this part over and over, Biff calling me Maynard and telling me that I, Maynard Chan, was the centre of attention, not him.

I looked at Henry Rendall. He was still grinning, but I figured he might be a little miffed I'd asked Biff Newsome for an autograph and not him, even though it was his show. I reached into my pocket, pulled out another sheet of paper and handed it to Henry Rendall.

He laughed and signed his name, using his own desk. I remembered why I was there and hiccuped again.

"Make that autograph to Julia Chan," I said as he started to hand the paper back to me. I don't think I'd ever said my mom's first name before. Now I'd said it on national television. "That's my mom. She's a real ... hic ... fan of yours, Mr. Rendall."

I figured it was a good idea to butter him up.

"And you're obviously not," he said, adding Mom's name to the sheet of paper.

I blushed and then hiccuped. "I've never even seen you before, sir. You're on too late at night."

I figured I should add something nice so, after a moment's pause I said, "You look like ... hic .. a nice guy, though."

The audience laughed and I smiled at them. They laughed again. Everything was going great. I relaxed a little.

"Any other autographs you want?" asked Henry Rendall.

I thought for a moment.

"Who's on later?"

"Nick Olsen."

The audience cheered.

"Who's Nick Olsen?" I asked, wrinkling my nose.

The audience laughed again, so I looked at them and shrugged. They laughed harder. I hiccuped. They laughed some more. Show business is crazy.

"He's a famous fashion designer," said Henry Rendall.

"Nah," I said, and the audience laughed loudly. "Who's on tomorrow night?" I asked, and Henry Rendall laughed for real, no pretend. I thought about pretend and hiccuped.

"Tell you what, Maynard," said Henry Rendall. "It's Friday now, but next week I will collect the autograph of each person on the show and send them all to you, promise."

The audience cheered.

"One thing I don't understand," I said.

"Yeah?"

"I've been hiccuping ... hic ... for three months, and nobody in my classroom laughs at me. Then ... hic ... I come on this show and no matter ... hic ... what I say, people think I'm hilarious. Why?"

"You are pretty funny," said Henry Rendall. "But we also have something your classroom doesn't. We have 'Laugh' and 'Clap' and 'Applaud' signs located where the audience can see them. Maybe classrooms should have them. George, put a camera on the signs. The signs light up when we need an audience reaction. We use the signs because some of our guests are boring. You're a smart boy, Maynard. What are you studying in school?"

The interview was over so quickly. Except for one short twelve-second period, I always remembered to hiccup. When my interview was over I didn't leave. I sat on the couch beside Biff Newsome and listened to Henry Rendall talk with the fashion designer. Naturally I had to keep hiccuping or people would notice. It drove the fashion designer crazy. Whenever he was ready with a funny line, I'd hiccup and the audience would laugh, without any sign lighting up. It was terrific.

Biff Newsome and Henry Rendall talked to each other during all the commercials. They didn't ignore me, either. Biff Newsome shook my hand again and Henry Rendall promised me he really would send an autograph book.

When the show was over, the band stopped playing and Henry Rendall sat back in his chair and rubbed his eyes. He wasn't grinning anymore. I couldn't stop hiccuping, though. I wasn't an entertainer who could relax when the stage lights were turned off. I was supposed to keep on being Hiccup Champion of the World.

AFTER YOU READ

Write a story

Think back to the funny situation in your own life. Write a story about what happened to you.

MEDIA CLOSE-UP

In this unit, you have learned how some media products are created. You also found out that knowing how the media is created can make you a better viewer. Now it is your turn to use all you have learned to make your own media product: a storyboard for a comic book.

BEFORE YOU BEGIN

Think about what you know about how comic books are made. You may want to go back and read "Red Raven: Comic Book Superhero" again. Ask yourself these questions:

- What kind of comic do I want to create?
- Who will be the main character?
- Where will my story take place?
- What will happen?
- Who will read my story?

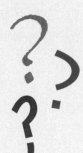

You may want to use a chart to organize your thoughts before you begin.

Here is an example of a chart that Suluxan used.

Main Character	boy
Other Characters	dog
Place Where Story Happens	living room
What Happens	boy tells dog to do tricks, dog doesn't do them, boy gets mad, boy leaves room, dog does tricks
Ending	boy comes back and dog pretends he can't do tricks

YOUR FIRST DRAFT

1. Make a Storyboard

- Use at least six frames.

- The frames can go either across or straight up and down.

- Sketch what will happen in each frame.

- Use a pencil because you might want to make changes.

Frames 1 and 2:	Introduce the characters and the place where the story happens.
Frames 3 and 4:	Tell about the problem that the main character faces.
Frames 5 and 6:	Tell how the character solves the problem.

TRY THIS!

Here is a rough sketch of Suluxan's storyboard.

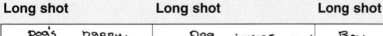

2. Set Up Your Shots

- Decide what kind of shot you will show in each frame.
- Include at least one long shot, one medium shot, and one close-up shot.

3. Think About Details

- Use expressive faces and sound effects. Symbols like a light bulb can show when a character has a new idea.

Remember you do not have much room to tell a story in a comic. Think about what you can do in each frame to help your reader understand the story better.

4. Add Your Text

- Decide what words will tell what is happening.
- Add speech bubbles or write sentences at the bottom of each frame.

5. Think About Colour

- Colour can also help the reader to understand what is happening in your comic. For example, yellow is usually a happy colour and black can be a sad colour.
- Make notes on your storyboard when you have thought about what colours you will use.

Here is one frame from Suluxan's finished comic.

REVISE AND EDIT

Go back and review your storyboard.

- Ask a classmate to look at your work. Listen to their suggestions. Are there ways to improve what you have done?
- Proofread your work for errors in spelling, punctuation, and grammar.

Create Your Comic

Take the information from your storyboard and draw the frames of your comic. Colour each frame. Share your comic with a classmate.

Think About Your Learning

Add your own ideas about what makes a good storyboard.

- Is there a main character?
- Does my story have a beginning, a middle, and an end?
- Have I used different shots: close-up, medium, and long?
- Did I use sound words and symbols to help tell my story?
- Did I use speech bubbles?
- Are my pictures big enough to see clearly? Is there enough detail?
- How did I use colour?

ACKNOWLEDGMENTS

Permission to reprint copyrighted material is gratefully acknowledged. Every effort has been made to trace ownership of all copyrighted material and to secure permission from copyright holders. In the event of any question arising as to the use of any material, we will be pleased to make the necessary corrections in future printings.

Photographs
Cover: K. Lothe/First Light; p. 7 William Belsey; p. 52 (top) SOVFOTO/EASTFOTO; p. 52 (bottom) used by permission of Dragana Panic; pp. 57-58, 63 (bottom) William Belsey; p. 65 courtesy of George T. Cunningham Elementary School; pp. 78-79 E. A. Hunter/NWP; pp. 80-81 Dick Hemingway; pp. 82-83 Visuals Unlimited/N. Pecnik; pp. 88-89 Bob Semple; pp. 92-94 courtesy of the Niagara Parks Commission; p. 95 (top left, bottom) courtesy of the Niagara Parks Commission; pp. 97, 99, 101 courtesy of the Niagara Parks Commission; pp. 116-117 © Graham Osborne; p. 119 Satellite Photo of Greater Vancouver, processed by Pacific Geomatics Ltd. of South Surrey, B.C.; p. 120 © Graham Osborne; p. 121 (top left) Visuals Unlimited/Michael S. Quinton, (top right) Visuals Unlimited/William J. Weber, (bottom) Visuals Unlimited/Will Troyer; p. 122 © Graham Osborne; pp. 131, 135 courtesy of Charles Fiddler; p. 146 ReBoot is a registered trademark of Mainframe Entertainment, Inc. ReBoot and ReBoot Characters © 1997 Mainframe Entertainment, Inc. All Rights Reserved; p. 149-151 Dick Hemingway; p. 153 courtesy of Bob Gundu; p. 155 © 1995 Photofest; p. 156 (top) © 1997 Universal/MPTV, (bottom) courtesy of Sheridan College.

Illustrations
Cover: Todd Ryoji; pp. 6-7 William Roy Brownridge; p. 7 (top) Sheena Lott, (middle left) Jerry Pinkney, (middle) Quentin Blake, (bottom left) Susan Leopold, (bottom right) Raúl Colón; p. 9 Renée Cuthbertson; pp. 10-11 Quentin Blake; pp. 13-14, 16-18 Jerry Pinkney; pp. 21-22, 25-29, 30-31 William Roy Brownridge; pp. 32-39 Raúl Colón; pp. 40-43 Susan Leopold; pp. 44-51 Sheena Lott; pp. 54-55 Dusan Petricic; p. 56 courtesy of Leo Ussak Elementary School; p. 57 Ian Greener; pp. 59, 61, 62, 63 courtesy of Leo Ussak Elementary School; pp. 64-73 courtesy of George T. Cunningham. Elementary School; pp. 86-87 Johnny Wú; pp. 90-91 Bernadette Lau; p. 94 Ian Greener; pp. 100, 102, 104-107 Jack McMaster; pp. 109-110, 113-114 Celia Godkin; p. 118 Allan Moon; p. 123 Julie Greener; pp. 128-129 Stephen MacEachern; pp. 132-134 courtesy of Bold Ink Graphics; pp. 136-141 Dave Whamond; pp. 142-144 Kathryn Adams; p. 145 © Catapult Productions 1997; p. 146 ReBoot is a registered trademark of Mainframe Entertainment, Inc. ReBoot and ReBoot Characters © 1997 Mainframe Entertainment, Inc. All Rights Reserved. p. 147 Kathryn Adams; p. 150 Tina Holdcroft; p. 152 Allan Moon; p. 153 Brad Black; p. 154 Bruce Krever; pp. 158-159 Kim LaFave; pp. 160-161 Sean Dawdy; pp. 162-165 Ken Phipps; pp. 166-169 Richard Hockney; pp. 171-172, 175-176, 179, 180, 183 Tadeusz Majewski.

Text
"I Can" by Mari Evans. © Mari Evans, 1976. From *Pass it On: African American Poetry for Children,* selected by Wade Hudson. Scholastic Inc. "The Greatest" by Michael